The Battle of Oriskany
1777

The Battle of Oriskany

The Battle of Oriskany
1777
The Conflict for the Mohawk Valley During the American War of Independence

Ellis H. Roberts

LEONAUR

The Battle of Oriskany 1777
The Conflict for the Mohawk Valley
During the American War of Independence
by Ellis H. Roberts

First published under the title
The Battle of Oriskany

Leonaur is an imprint of Oakpast Ltd

Copyright in this form © 2011 Oakpast Ltd

ISBN: 978-0-85706-473-8 (hardcover)
ISBN: 978-0-85706-474-5 (softcover)

http://www.leonaur.com

Publisher's Notes

Contents

The Battle of Oriskany

The fault attaches to each of us, that the share of the valley of the Mohawk in the events which gave birth and form to the American republic, is not better understood. Our prosperity has been so steady and so broad that we have looked forward rather than backward. Other States, other parts of the country, have been recalling the scenes which render their soil classic, and from the end of the century summoning; back the men and the deeds of its beginning. A duty long neglected falls upon those whose lot is cast here in Central New York. These hills and these valleys in perennial eloquence proclaim the story of prowess and of activity.

To translate from them, to gather the scattered threads of chronicle and tradition, to hold the place that has been fairly won by the Mohawk valley, is a task which has yet been only partially done. Some time or other it will be fulfilled, for achievements have a voice which mankind delights to hear. The privilege of this hour is to revive the memories and to celebrate the heroism of the Battle of Oriskany.[1] Without anything of narrow local pride, with calm eye and steady judgment, not ashamed to praise where praise was earned, nor unwilling to admit weakness where weakness existed, let us recall that deadly fight, and measure its significance and its relations to the continental strife in which our republic was born.

---

1. See Appendix, for the derivation and orthography.

1

The Situation Before the Battle

For in the autumn of 1777, it was clear that the American colonies were fighting not for rights under the British crown, but for free and separate life. The passionate outbursts of 1775 had discharged their thunder and lightning. The guns of Lexington had echoed round the world. The brilliant truths of the Declaration had for a year blazed over the battlefields of the infant nation. They had been hallowed by defeat; for Montgomery had fallen at Quebec, Sullivan had met with disasters at Flatbush, the British occupied New York, and Washington had retreated through the Jerseys, abandoning Long Island and the Lower Hudson. Sir Guy Carleton had swept over Lake Champlain, fortunately not holding his conquest, and Burgoyne had captured the noted stronghold Ticonderoga.

But the nation had also tasted victory. In the dread December days of 1776, Washington had checked the tide of despair by his gallant assault at Trenton, and General Howe had been forced to concentrate his army against Philadelphia. Boston had seen its last of the soldiers of George the Third. Better than all, the States were everywhere asserting their vitality. Far off Tennessee indignant at his use of Indians in war, had taken sides against the British king. Georgia had promised if Britain destroyed her towns, that her people would retire into the forests. The splendid defence of Fort Moultrie had saved Charleston and proved South Carolina's zeal for the republic which it was afterwards to assail. Virginia had furnished many of the civil leaders and the commander-in-chief to the republic, and had formally struck the British flag which had floated over its State house.

If Maryland hesitated, New Jersey joined hands with Pennsylvania and New York, and all New England had pledged itself to the contest which it had begun. In New York as well as in other States, a State constitution had been adopted, and George Clinton had been inaugurated as Governor at the close of that disastrous July. The tide of battle surged wildest in that critical summer in Northern New York. So in trying hours, the blood courses most swiftly at the heart. Great results were expected. The British fleet sailed up the Hudson. A British general, favourite of the muses, and in after years notable fortunate,[1] came down Lake Champlain to meet it at Albany. A column formidable in its elements and led by a commander chosen by the king for the purpose, was to come from the north and west to complete the irresistible triad. Tory bands were ravaging the country southward in Schoharie and towards Kingston,[2] Cause of alarm there was to the patriots; ground of confidence to the invaders. The war hung on the events in this field; and the scales of destiny inclined to the side of the king.

The combatants had learned to understand each other. The burning words of Junius had long rankled in the British mind. Burke's magnificent plea for conciliation had borne no fruit. Chatham had two years before "rejoiced that America had resisted," and told the ministers they could not conquer America, and cripple as he was he cried out: "I might as soon think of driving the colonies before me with this crutch;" but in the next spring he still clung to the hope that Britain would yet prevent separation. The insolence of Lord North had shattered the unanimity which King George boasted the Declaration had produced, and Fox had said if the dilemma were between conquering and abandoning America, he was for abandoning America.

---

1. General Burgoyne before the war sat in Parliament. He was agreeable and clever as a dramatic poet. He became commander-in-chief of the British forces in Ireland.
2. J. R. Simms has clearly fixed the date of these raids, in the summer of 1777, (see his *History of Schoharie county* and *Border Wars of New York*,) and not in 1778, as stated in Campbell's Annals of Tryon County.

The citizens of London had appealed to the King to stop the "unnatural and unfortunate war." General Howe had already written to his brother, (April 2, 1777,) "my hopes of terminating the war this year are vanished." In Britain, wise men had learned that the war would be desperate. In America the magnitude of the contest was felt. The alliance of France had been diligently sought, and LaFayette had arrived and been appointed major general, while Kalb's offer had not been accepted. More than one general had been tried and found wanting in capacity, and the jealousies of the camp were working mischief. The financial burdens weighed heavily, and paper money had begun its downward career. Criticism of Washington's slowness was heard, and speculators were making profit of the country's necessities.

Bounties had been offered and the draft employed for raising troops. The loyalists were making the most of the hardships. The land was rocking in "times that try men's souls." The earlier part of the military campaign of 1777 had not been propitious to the patriots. The darkness rested especially on New York. Burgoyne had penetrated from Canada to the Hudson with the loss of only two hundred men. Clinton from the bay threatened to advance up the river, as he finally did, but fortunately not at the critical moment. The success of the corps moving inland from Oswego, would shatter the centre of the American position.

THE OBJECT OF THE CAMPAIGN OF 1777.

The fight was for the continent. The strategy embraced the lines from Boston to the mouth of the Chesapeake, from Montreal even to Charleston. Montgomery's invasion of Canada, although St. John's and Montreal were taken, failed before Quebec, and the retreat of the American forces gave Burgoyne the base for his comprehensive campaign. Howe had been compelled to give up New England, which contained nearly one-third of the population and strength of the colonies. The centre of attack and of defence was the line of New York and Philadelphia. From their foothold at New York, on the one hand, and Montreal on the other, the British commanders aimed to grind the patriots of the Mohawk valley between the upper and nether millstones.

The design was to cut New England off from the other States, and to seize the country between the Hudson and Lake Ontario as the vantage ground for sweeping and decisive operations. This was the purpose of the wedge which Burgoyne sought to drive through the heart of the Union. In the beginning of that fateful August, Howe held all the country about New York, including the islands, and the Hudson up to Peekskill; the British forces also commanded the St. Lawrence and Lake Ontario, and their southern shores, finding no opposition north of the Mohawk and Saratoga lake. The junction of Howe and Burgoyne would have rendered their armies masters of the key to the military position.

This strip of country from the Highlands of the Hudson to the head of the Mohawk, was the sole shield against such concentration of British power. Once lost it would become a sword to cut the patriots into fragments. They possessed it by no certain tenure. Two months later Governor Clinton and General Putnam lost their positions on the Hudson. Thus far Burgoyne's march had been one of conquest. His capture of Ticonderoga had startled the land. The frontier fort at the head of the Mohawk was to cost him the column on whose march he counted so much.

Fort Stanwix and its Garrison.

Fort Stanwix[3] (known in this campaign to the patriots as Fort Schuyler,) was built in 1758 against the French. The next year, the French met with those disasters which in 1760, gave Canada to the English, and thereafter Fort Stanwix served only for purposes of Indian trade, and as a protection to the carry between the Mohawk and Wood Creek. It had been a favourite place for peaceful meeting with the Indians.[4] Naturally it had lost its military strength, and when in April, 1777, Colonel Gansevoort occupied it with the third regiment of the New York line, it was sadly out of repair. The plans for its reconstruction were yet in

---

3 & 4 See Appendix.

progress when St. Leger appeared before it. But care and labour had been so effectual that the broken walls had been restored, and the ruins which the invader came to overrun had given place to defences too strong for his attack.

Col. Peter Gansevoort, who was in command, was a native of Albany, now twenty-eight years of age. He had been with Montgomery before Quebec, and there won his rank as colonel. His conduct here was admirable. The courage of youth did not prevent on his part a wisdom worthy of much riper years. With him as Lieutenant Colonel was Marinus Willett, a native of New York city, aged thirty-seven, trained in the French war and the invasion of Canada, a dashing soldier, ready for any adventure, and shrewd in all the ways of border war. He had been in the expedition for which the fort had been erected, and now helped to save it.

The Chaplain of the garrison was Samuel Kirkland, that sainted missionary to the Six Nations, to whom Central New York is so much indebted in every way. He was probably absent at the time, on service for the Congress, for he was trusted and employed on important missions by the patriot leaders.[5]

The garrison consisted of seven hundred and fifty men. It was composed of Gansevoort's own regiment, the Third New York, with two hundred men under Lieutenant Colonel Mellon of Colonel Wesson's regiment of the Massachusetts line. Colonel Mellon had fortunately arrived with a convoy of boats filled with supplies, on the second of August, when the enemy's fires were already in sight only a mile away. This was the force with which Gansevoort was to hold the fort.

The British advance appeared on the second of August. The investiture was complete on the fourth. The siege was vigorously prosecuted on the fifth, but the cannon "had not the least effect on the sod-work of the fort," and "the royals had only the power of teasing."[6]

---

5. See Lothrop's *Life of Kirkland. Lectures by William Tracy.*
6. St. Leger's *Narrative in Burgoyne's Defence*, given in the tenth section of this Appendix.

13

The corps before Fort Stanwix was formidable in every element of military strength. The expedition with which it was charged, was deemed by the war secretary at Whitehall of the first consequence, and it had received as marked attention as any army which King George ever let loose upon the colonists. For its leader Lieutenant Colonel Barry St. Leger had been chosen by the king himself, on Burgoyne's nomination. He deserved the confidence, if we judge by his advance, by his precautions, by his stratagem at Oriskany, and the conduct of the siege, up to the panic at the rumour that Arnold was coming. In the regular army of England he became an ensign in 1756, and coming to America the next year he had served in the French war, and learned the habits of the Indians, and of border warfare.

In some local sense, perhaps as commanding this corps, he was styled a brigadier. His regular rank was Lieutenant Colonel of the thirty-fourth regiment. In those days of trained soldiers it was a marked distinction to be chosen to select an independent corps on important service. A wise commander, fitted for border war, his order of march bespeaks him. Skilful in affairs, and scholarly in accomplishments, his writings prove him. Prompt, tenacious, fertile in resources, attentive to detail, while master of the whole plan, he would not fail where another could have won.

Inferior to St. Leger in rank, but superior to him in natural powers and in personal magnetism, was Joseph Brant—Thayendanegea—chief of the Mohawks. He had been active in arraying the Six Nations on the side of King George, and only the Oneidas and Tuscaroras had refused to follow his lead. He was now thirty-five years of age; in figure the ideal Indian, tall and spare and lithe and quick; with all the genius of his tribe, and the training gained in Connecticut schools, and in the family of Sir William Johnson; he had been a lion in London, and flattered at British headquarters in Montreal. Among the Indians he was pre-eminent, and in any circle he would have been conspicuous.

As St. Leger represented the regular army of King George, and Brant the Indian allies, Sir John Johnson led the regiments which had been organized from the settlers in the Mohawk Valley. He had inherited from his father, Sir William, the largest estate held on the continent by any individual, William Penn excepted. He had early taken sides with the King against the colonists, and having entered into a compact with the patriots to preserve peace and remain at Johnstown, he had violated his promise, and fled to Canada. He came now with a sense of personal wrong, to recover his possessions and to resume the almost royal sway which he had exercised. He at this time held a commission as colonel in the British army, to raise and command forces raised among the loyalists of the valley.

Besides these was Butler—John Butler, a brother-in-law of Johnson; lieutenant colonel by rank, rich and influential in the valley, familiar with the Indians and a favourite with them, shrewd and daring and savage, already the father of that son Walter who was to be the scourge of the settlers, and with him to render ferocious and bloody the border war. He came from Niagara, and was now in command of Tory rangers.

The forces were like the leaders. It has been the custom to represent St. Leger's army as a "motley crowd." [7] On the contrary it was a picked force, especially designated by orders from headquarters in Britain.[8] He enumerates his "artillery, the thirty-fourth and the King's regiment, with the Hessian riflemen and the whole corps of Indians," with him, while his advance consisting of a detachment under Lieutenant Bird, had gone before, and "the rest of the army, led by Sir John Johnson," was a day's march in the rear. Johnson's whole regiment[9] was with him together with Butler's Tory rangers, with at least one company of Canadians.[10] The country from Schoharie westward had been scoured of loyalists to add to this column. For such an expedition, the force could not have been better chosen.

---

7. Lossing's *Field-Book*, vol. 1. Irving's *Washington*, vol. 3.
8. See Appendix, for the official order designating the troops.
9. *British Annual Register* for 1877. See the fourteenth section of this Appendix.
10. *Impartial History*, (London, 1780.)

The pet name of the "King's regiment" is significant. The artillery was such as could be carried by boat, and adapted to the sort of war before it. It had been especially designated from Whitehall.[11] The Hanau *Chasseurs* were trained and skilful soldiers. The Indians were the terror of the land. The Six Nations had joined the expedition in full force[12] except the Oneidas and the Tuscaroras. With the latter tribes the influence of Samuel Kirkland had over-borne that of the Johnsons, and the Oneidas and the Tuscaroras were by their peaceful attitude more than by hostility useful to Congress to the end. [13] The statement[14] that two thousand Canadians accompanied him as axemen, is no doubt an exaggeration; but exclusive of such helpers and of non-combatants, the corps counted not less than seventeen hundred fighting men.[15]

King George could not then have sent a column better fitted for its task, or better equipped, or abler led, or more intent on achieving all that was imposed upon it. Leaving Montreal, it started on the nineteenth of July from Buck Island, its rendezvous at the entrance of Lake Ontario. It had reached Fort Stanwix without the loss of a man, as if on a summer's picnic. It had come through in good season. Its chief never doubted that he would make quick work with the fort. He had even cautioned Lieutenant Bird who led the advance, lest he should risk the seizure with his unaided detachment. When his full force

---

11. *Burgoyne's State of the Expedition*, and section fourth of this Appendix.
12. Colonel Guy Johnson wrote, November 11, 1777, to Lord Germain, "The greater part of those from the Six Nations with my officers in that country, joined General St. Leger's troops and Sir John Johnson's provincials, and were principally concerned in the action near Fort Stanwix." *Colonial History of New York*, vol. 8. This was in accordance with a dispatch from Brant to Sir Guy, in June or July, that the "Six Nations were all in readiness, (the Oneidas excepted,) and all determined, as they expressed it, to act as one man." *Colonial History*, vol. 8.
13. William Tracy in his lectures, gives much credit for this result to James Dean. See Appendix, for a characteristic letter of Rev. Samuel Kirkland.
14. Dawson's *Battles of the United States*.
15. *Gordon's History*, (London, 1787,) vol. 2, says St. Leger's "whole force did not probably exceed 800 men:" he credits him with "700 Indian warriors," This is loose talk. President Dwight, (*Travels*, vol. 3,) who visited Fort Stanwix in 1799, places the number from 1,500 to 1,800.

appeared, his faith was sure that the fort would "fall without a single shot."[16] So confident was he that he sent a dispatch to Burgoyne on the fifth of August, assuring him that the fort would be his directly, and they would speedily meet as victors at Albany.[17] General Schuyler had in an official letter expressed a like fear.[18]

THE PATRIOT RISING IN TRYON COUNTY.

St. Leger was therefore surprised as well as annoyed by the news that the settlers on the Mohawk had been aroused, and were marching in haste to relieve the fort. He found that his path to join Burgoyne was to be contested. He watched by skilful scouts the gathering of the patriots; their quick and somewhat irregular assembling; he knew of their march from Fort Dayton, and their halt at Oriskany. Brant[19] told him that they advanced, as brave, untrained militia, without throwing out skirmishers, and with Indian guile the Mohawk chose the pass in which an ambush should be set for them. The British commander guarded the way for several miles from his position, by scouts within speaking distance of each other. He knew the importance of his movement, and he was guilty of no neglect.

THE AMBUSCADE.

From his camp at Fort Stanwix St. Leger saw all, and directed all. Sir John Johnson[20] led the force thrown out to meet the patriots, with Butler as his second, but Brant was its controlling head. The Indians were most numerous; "the whole corps," a "large body," St. Leger testifies. And with the Indians he reports were "some troops." The presence of Johnson, and of Butler, as well as

16. Colonel Claus had so promised the Indians. Campbell's *Annals of Tryon County*. Upon Arnold's approach, when St. Leger urged the Indiana to stay, the chiefs replied: "When we marched down, you told us there would be no fighting for us Indians; we might go down and smoke our pipes; but now a number of our warriors have been killed, and you mean to sacrifice us." Thacher's *Military Journal*.
17. Logging's *Field-Book of the Revolution*, vol. 1.
18. See Appendix, for an extract from the letter.
19. The information came on the fifth from Brant's sister, who was a mistress of Sir William Johnson. See Claus' letter in the Appendix.
20. See Appendix, for proof that Johnson actually led the British at Oriskany.

of Claus and Watts, of Captains Wilson, Hare and McDonald,[21] the chief loyalists of the valley, proves that their followers were in the fight. Butler [22] refers to the New Yorkers whom we know as Johnson's Greens, and the Rangers, as in the engagement in large numbers. St. Leger was under the absolute necessity of preventing the patriot force from attacking him in the rear. He could not do less than send every available man out to meet it. Quite certainly the choicest of the army were taken from the dull duty of the siege for this critical operation. They left camp at night and lay above and around the ravine at Oriskany, in the early morning of the sixth of August. They numbered not less than twelve hundred men under chosen cover.

GENERAL HERKIMER'S RALLY.

The coming of St. Leger had been known in the valley for weeks. Burgoyne had left Montreal in June, and the expedition by way of Lake Ontario, as the experience of a hundred years prophesied, would respond to his advance. Colonel Gansevoort had appealed to the Committee of Safety for Tryon county, for help. Its chairman was Nicholas Herchkeimer, (known to us as Herkimer,) who had been appointed a brigadier general by Congress in the preceding autumn.[23] His family was large, and it was divided in the contest. A brother was captain with Sir John Johnson, and a brother-in-law was one of the chief of the loyalists. He was now forty-eight years of age,[24] short, slender, of dark complexion, with black hair and bright eyes.[25] He had German pluck and leadership, but he had also German caution and deliberation. He foresaw the danger, and had given warning

21. Captain McDonald of Johnson's Greens, and Captains Wilson and Hare of the Rangers, are reported by Colonel Butler among the killed. Other captains must have been on the field. While the title was perhaps loosely used, it signifies prominence, and some followers.

22. Stone's *Life of Brant.*

23. Stone's *Life of Brant,* vol. 1. His commission to this rank by the New York convention, bearing date September 5, 1776, is in the possession of the Oneida Historical Society, at Utica.

24. Benton's *Herkimer County.*

25. Newspaper report of tradition in the Wagner family.

to General Schuyler at Albany.

On the seventeenth of July he had issued a proclamation, announcing that the enemy, two thousand strong, was at Oswego, and that as soon as he should approach, every male person being in health, and between sixteen and sixty years of age, should immediately be ready to march against him. Tryon County had strong appeals for help also from Cherry Valley and Unadilla, and General Herkimer had been southward at the close of June to check operations of the Tories and Indians under Brant. The danger from this direction delayed and obstructed recruiting for the column against St. Leger.

The stress was great, and Herkimer was bound to keep watch south as well as west. He waited only to learn where need was greatest, and he went thither. On the thirtieth of July, a letter from Thomas Spencer, a half-breed Oneida, read on its way to General Schuyler, made known the advance of St. Leger. Herkimer's order was promptly issued,[26] and soon brought in eight hundred men. They were nearly all by blood Germans and low Dutch, with a few of other nationalities.

The roster [27] so far as can now be collected, indicates the presence of persons of English, Scotch, Irish, Welsh and French blood, but these are exceptions, and the majority of the force was beyond question German. They gathered from their farms and clearings, carrying their equipments with them. They met at Fort Dayton, near the mouth of the West Canada Creek. This post was held at the time by a part of Colonel Wesson's Massachusetts regiment,[28] also represented in the garrison at Fort Stanwix.

The little army was divided into four regiments or battalions. The first, which Herkimer had once commanded, was now led

---

26. All authorities agree that on receipt of Spencer's letter, Herkimer acted vigorously. Stone's *Brant* ; *Annals of Tryon County* ; Ramsey's *History of the Revolution*, (1789.) vol. 2, "collected" his men by the third of August; Lossing's *Field-Book*, vol. 1; Benton's *History of Herkimer County*.
27. See Appendix, for a roster collected with much care by the *Utica Herald*, in July, 1877.
28. Benton's *Herkimer County*.

by Colonel Ebenezer Cox, and was from the district of Canajoharie; of the second, from Palatine, Jacob Klock was colonel;
the third was under Colonel Frederick Visscher, and came from
Mohawk; the fourth, gathered from German Flats and Kingsland, Peter Bellinger commanded.[29]

GENERAL HERKIMER'S ADVANCE.

Counsels were divided whether they should await further
accessions, or hasten to Fort Stanwix. Prudence prompted delay. St. Leger's force was more than double that of Herkimer; it
might be divided, and while one-half occupied the patriot column, the Indians under Tory lead might hurry down the valley,
gathering reinforcements while they ravaged the homes of the
patriots. The blow might come from Unadilla, where Brant had
been as late as the early part of that very July. Herkimer, at Fort
Dayton, was in position to turn in either direction. But the way
of the Mohawk was the natural and traditional warpath. The
patriots looked to Fort Stanwix as their defence. They started
on the fourth, crossed the Mohawk where is now Utica, and
reached Whitestown on the fifth. Here it was probably that a
band of Oneida Indians joined the column.

From this point or before, Herkimer sent an express to Colonel Gansevoort arranging for co-operation. He was to move
forward when three cannon signalled that aid was ready. The
signal was not heard; the messengers had been delayed. His chief
advisers, including Colonel Cox and Paris, the latter a mem-
ber of the committee of Safety, urged quicker movements. Fort
Stanwix might fall, while they were delaying, and the foe could
then turn upon them. Herkimer was taunted as a coward and a
Tory. His German phlegm was stirred. He warned his impatient
advisers that they would be the first in the face of the enemy to
flee. He gave the order "march on!" Apprised of the ambuscade,
his courage which had been assailed prevented the necessary
precautions.

---

29. *Calendar of New York Manuscripts*, vol. 1, (revised.) See in connection with the
roster in the Appendix, the territory covered by these districts.

HERKIMER AT THE BATTLE OF ORISKANY

He led his little band on. If he had before been cautious, now he was audacious. His course lay on the south side of the river, avoiding its bends, where the country loses the general level which the rude road sought to follow, when it could be found. For three or four miles hills rose upon valleys, with occasional gulleys. The trickling springs and the spring freshets had cut more than one ravine where even in the summer, the water still moistened the earth. These run towards the river, from southerly towards the north. Corduroy roads had been constructed over the marshes, for this was the line of such travel as sought Fort Stanwix and the river otherwise than by boat.

Herkimer had come to one of the deepest of these ravines, ten or twelve rods wide, running narrower up to the hills at the south, and broadening towards the Mohawk into the flat bottom land. Where the forests were thick, where the rude roadway ran down into the marsh, and the ravine closed like a pocket, he pressed his way. Not in soldierly order, not watching against the enemy, but in rough haste, the eight hundred marched. They reached the ravine at ten in the morning. The advance had gained the higher ground.

Then as so often, the woods became alive. Black eyes flashed from behind every tree. Rifles blazed from a thousand unexpected coverts. The Indians rushed out hatchet in hand, decked in paint and feathers. The brave band was checked. It was cut in two. The assailants aimed first of all to seize the supply train. Colonel Visscher, who commanded its guard, showed his courage before and after[30] and doubtless fought well here, as the best informed descendants of other heroes of the battle believe. But his regiment was driven northward towards the river, was cut up or in great part captured with the supplies and ammunition.

In the ravine and just west of it, Herkimer rallied those who stood with him. Back to back, shoulder to shoulder, they faced the foe. Where shelter could be had, two stood together, so that one might fire while the other loaded. Often the fight grew

---

30. Stone's *Life of Brant*, vol. 2.

closer, and the knife ended the personal contest. Eye to eye, hand to hand, this was a fight of men. Nerve and brawn and muscle, were the price of life. Rifle and knife, spear and tomahawk were the only weapons, or the clubbed butt of the rifle. It was not a test of science, not a weighing of enginery, not a measure of calibre nor an exhibition of choicest mechanism. Men stood against death, and death struck at them with the simplest implements.

Homer sings of chariots and shields. Here were no such helps, no such defences. Forts or earthworks, barricades or abattis, there were none. The British force had chosen its ground. Two to one it must have been against the band which stood and fought in that pass, forever glorious. Herkimer, early wounded and his horse shot under him, sat on his saddle beneath a beech tree, just where the hill rises at the west a little north of the centre of the ravine, calmly smoking a pipe while ordering the battle. He was urged to retire from so much danger; his reply is the eloquence of a hero: "I will face the enemy."

The ground tells the story of the fight. General Herkimer was with the advance, which had crossed the ravine. His column stretched out for nearly half a mile. Its head was a hundred rods or more west of the ravine, his rear-guard reached as far east of it. The firing began from the hills into the gulf. Herkimer closed his line on its centre, and in reaching that point his white horse was shot under him. The flag-staff today on the hill marks his position. Then as today, (at time of first publication), the hills curved like a scimitar, from the west to the east on the north side of the river. Fort Stanwix could not be seen but it lay in the plain just beyond the gap in the hills, six miles distant.

The Mohawk from the mouth of the Oriskany curved northward, so that here it is as far away in a right line, perhaps a mile in each case. The bottoms were marshy, as they yet are where the trees exclude the sun. Now the New York Central Railroad and the Erie Canal mark the general direction of the march of the patriots from their starting-place hither. Then forests of beach and birch and maple and hemlock covered the land where now orchards and rich meadows extend, and grain-fields are ripening for the harvest. Even the forests are gone, and the Mohawk and the hills and the ravine and "Battle Brook," are the sole witnesses to confirm the traditions which have come down to us. The elms which fling their plumes to the sky, are young successors to the knightly warriors who were once masters here. Through the forests Herkimer from his elevation could cate the general outlines of the battle. Some of his advance had fallen at the farthest point to which they had marched. Upon their left, the enemy had appeared in force, and had closed up from the southward, and on the east side of the ravine. The patriots had been pushed to the north side of the road, away from the line which the corduroy still marks in the ravine, and those who tied sought the river.

Skeletons have been found in the smaller ravine about two hundred rods west, and at the mouth of the Oriskany, an extent of a mile and a half; and gun-barrels and other relics along the line of the Erie Canal, and down towards the river. These are witnesses of the limits of the battle. They mark the centre here. Here gathered the brave militia without uniforms, in the garb of farmers, for their firesides and their homes, and the republic just born which was to be. Against them here, in the ravine, pursuing and capturing the rear-guard on the east of the ravine or down in it, and thence towards the river, rushed from the forests, uniformed and well equipped, Johnson's Greens in their gay colour, the German Chasseurs, Europe's best soldiers, with picked men of British and Canadian regiments, and the Indian warriors decked in the equipments with which they made war brilliant.

Some of this scene, Herkimer saw; some of it extent of space and thickness of forest hid from his eye. But here he faced the enemy, and here he ordered the battle. During the carnage, a storm of wind and rain and lightning brought a respite. Old men preserve the tradition that in the path by which the enemy came, a broad windfall was cut, and was seen for long years afterwards. The elements caused only a short lull. In came at the thick of the strife, a detachment of Johnson's Greens; and they sought to appear reinforcements for the patriots.

They paid dearly for the fraud, for thirty were quickly killed. Captain Gardenier slew three with his spear, one after the other.[31] Captain Dillenback assailed by three, brained one, shot the second, and bayoneted the third. Henry Thompson grew faint with hunger, sat down on the body of a dead soldier, ate his lunch, and refreshed resumed the fight. William Merckley, mortally wounded, to a friend offering to assist him, said: "Take care of yourself, leave me to my fate." [32]

Such men could not be whipped. The Indians finding they were losing many, became suspicious that their allies wished to destroy them, and fired on them, giving unexpected aid to the patriot band.[33] Tradition relates that an Oneida maid, only fifteen years old, daughter of a chief, fought on the side of the patriots, firing her rifle, and shouting her battle cry. [34] The Indians raised the cry of retreat, "*Oonah!*" "*Oonah!*" Johnson heard the firing; of a sortie from the fort. The British fell back, after five hours of desperate fight. J Herkimer and his gallant men held the ground.

The Sortie

The sortie from Fort Stanwix which Herkimer expected, was made as soon as his messengers arrived. They were delayed, and yet got through at a critical moment. Colonel Willett made a sally at the head of two hundred and fifty men, totally routed two of the enemy's encampments, and captured their contents, including five British flags. The exploit did not cost a single patriot life, while at least six of the enemy were killed and four made prisoners. It aided to force the British retreat from Oriskany. The captured flags were floated beneath the stars and stripes,

31. Stone's *Life of Brant*, vol. 1.

32. Simms' *Schoharie*.

33. President Dwight (*Travels*, vol. 3,) who in 1799, heard the stories of persons living near the battlefield, relates this incident.

34. Newspaper report of a tradition in the family of George Wagner, a survivor.

35. Dr. Moses Younglove, who was taken prisoner at the battle, fixes the time: *Then we with equal fury joined the fight Ere Phoebus gained his full meridian height, Nor ceased the horrors of the bloody fray, Till lie had journeyed half his evening way.* Appendix to Campbell's *Annals of Tryon County*.

fashioned in the fort from cloaks and shirts; and here for the first time the flag of the republic was raised in victory over British colours.[36]

THE LOSSES.

The slaughter at Oriskany was terrible. St. Leger claims that four hundred of Herkimer's men were killed and two hundred captured, leaving only two hundred to escape. No such number of prisoners was ever accounted for. The Americans admitted two hundred killed, one-fourth of the whole army. St. Leger places the number of Indians killed at thirty, and the like number wounded, including favourite chiefs and confidential warriors.

It was doubtless greater, for the Senecas alone lost thirty-six killed, and in all the tribes twice as many must have been killed. St. Leger makes no account of any of his whites killed or wounded. Butler,[37] however, mentions of New Yorkers (Johnson's Greens) killed, Captain McDonald; Captain Watts dangerously wounded and one subaltern. Of the Tory Rangers Captains Wilson and Hare (their chiefs after Butler) were killed. With such loss of officers, the death list of privates must have been considerable. The Greens alone lost thirty. In Britain it was believed as many of the British were killed by the Indians as by the militia[38]

The loss of British and Indians must have approached a hundred and fifty killed. Eye-witnesses were found who estimated it as great as that of the Americans. [39] The patriot dead included Colonel Cox, and his Lieutenant Colonel Hunt, Majors Eisenlord, Van Slyck, Klapsattle and Blevin; and Captains Diefendorf,

---

36. Lossing, *Field-Book*, vol. 1, says the blue was taken from a camlet cloak of Captain Swartwout, and the white from cotton shirts. General Schuyler Hamilton in the *Historical Magazine*, for July, 1877, states on the authority of his grandmother, a daughter of General Philip Schuyler, that the stripes were made from a scarlet cloak belonging to one of the women of the garrison. Willett says the blue cloak had been captured from the *British at Peekskill; Narrative*. All that relates to this flag, the first ever lifting the stars and stripes in battle and in victory, has lasting interest.
37. Claus agrees substantially, and speaks of two or three privates killed. Letter to Secretary Knox, in London; *New York Colonial History*, vol. 8, see this Appendix.
38. Gordon's *History*, (London, 1787,) vol. 2.
39. A. D. Quackenboss who was in the fight so believed. Stone's *Brant*; Neilson's *Burgoyne*.

Crouse, Bowman, Dillenback, Davis, Pettengill, Helmer, Graves and Fox; with no less than four members of the Tryon county committee of Safety, who were present as volunteers. They were Isaac Paris, Samuel Billington, John Dygert, and Jacob Snell. Spencer, the Oneida, who gave the warning to the patriots, was also among the killed. The heads of the patriot organization in the valley were swept off. Herkimer's glory is that out of such slaughter he snatched the substance of victory. In no other battle of the revolution did the ratio of deaths rise so high. At Waterloo, the French loss was not in so large a ratio to the number engaged, as was Herkimer's at Oriskany; nor did the allies suffer as much on that bloody field.

Frightful barbarities were wreaked on the bodies of the dead, and on the prisoners who fell into the hands of the Indians. The patriots held the field at the close of the fight, and were able to carry off their wounded. Among these was the brave and sturdy Herkimer, who was taken on a litter of boughs to his home, and after suffering the amputation of his leg, died on the sixteenth of August, like a Christian hero. Of the dead some at least lay unburied until eighteen days later. Arnold's column rendered to them that last service. [40]

After the battle, Colonel Samuel Campbell[41] afterwards conspicuous in Otsego County, became senior officer, and organized the shattered patriots, leading them in good order back to Fort Dayton. The night of the fight, they bivouacked at Utica. Terrible as their losses had been, only sixteen days later Governor Clinton positively ordered them to join General Arnold on his expedition with one-half of each regiment. [42] In his desperation, Sir John Johnson "proposed to march down the country with about two hundred men," and Claus would have added Indians;[43] but St. Leger disapproved of the suggestion. Only a

40. Jones' *History of Oneida County*; Tracy's *Lectures*.
41. Letter of his grandson, Hon. W. W. Campbell, in *Utica Herald*, July 27, 1877.
42. See Appendix, for this important letter, which is copied from the manuscript in the State Library at Albany.
43. Claus' letter to Knox; *London Documents in Colonial History*, vol. 8, and section seventeenth of this Appendix.

raid could have been possible. The fighting capacity of St. Leger's army was exhausted at Oriskany, and he knew it.

THE SIEGE. [44]

St. Leger's advance was checked. His junction with Burgoyne was prevented. The rising of loyalists in the valley did not occur. He claimed indeed the "completest victory" at Oriskany. He notified the garrison that Burgoyne was victorious at Albany, and demanded peremptorily the surrender of the fort, threatening that prolonged resistance would result in general massacre at the hands of the enraged Indians. Johnson, Claus and Butler issued an address to the inhabitants of Tryon County, urging them to submit, because "surrounded by victorious armies." Colonel Gansevoort treated the summons as an insult, and held his post with sturdy steadiness."[45] The people of the valley sided with Congress against the King. For sixteen days after Oriskany, St. Leger lay before Fort Stanwix, and heard more and more clearly the rumbles of fresh resistance from the valley.

THE RELIEF UNDER ARNOLD'S LEAD

Colonel Willett who led the gallant sortie, accompanied by Major Stockwell, risked no less danger on a mission through thickets and hidden foes, to inform General Schuyler at Albany of the situation. In a council of officers, bitter opposition arose to Schuyler's proposal to send relief to Fort Stanwix, on the plea that it would weaken the army at Albany, the more important position. Schuyler was equal to the occasion,, acting promptly, and with great energy. "Gentlemen," said he, "I take the responsibility upon myself. Where is the brigadier who will command the relief? I shall beat up for volunteers tomorrow."[46] Benedict Arnold, then unstained by treason, promptly offered to lead the army.

---

44. For a sketch of the siege of Fort Stanwix presented to Colonel Gansevoort by L. Fleury, and with a map of the village of Rome overlaid upon it, see Hough's Memoir of M. Pouchot.

45. The British Impartial History says "Colonel Gansevoort behaved with great firmness."

46. Lossing's *Life of Schuyler*.

On the next day, August ninth,[47] eight hundred volunteers were enrolled, chiefly of General Larned's Massachusetts brigade. General Israel Putnam ordered the regiments of Colonel Cortlandt and Livingston from Peekskill to join the relief "against those worse than infernals."[48] Arnold was to take supplies wherever he could get them, and especially not to offend the already unfriendly Mohawks. Schuyler enjoined upon him also "as the inhabitants of Tryon County were chiefly Germans, it might be well to praise their bravery at Oriskany, and ask their gallant aid in the enterprise." Arnold reached Fort Dayton, and on the twentieth of August issued as commander-in-chief of the army of the United States of America on the Mohawk River, a characteristic proclamation, denouncing St. Leger as "a leader of a *banditti* of robbers, murderers and traitors, composed of savages of America and more savage Britons." The militia joined him in great numbers. On the twenty-second, Arnold pushed forward, and on the twenty-fourth he arrived at Fort Stanwix. St. Leger had raised the siege and precipitately fled.

St. Leger had been frightened by rumours of the rapid advance of Arnold's army. Arnold had taken pains to fill the air with them. He had sent to St. Leger's camp a half-witted loyalist, Hon Yost Schuyler, to exaggerate his numbers and his speed. The Indians in camp were restive and kept track of the army of relief. They badgered St. Leger to retreat, and threatened to abandon him. They raised the alarm, "they are coming!" and for the numbers of the patriots approaching, they pointed to the leaves of the forest.

ST. LEGER'S FLIGHT.

On the twenty-second of August, while Arnold was yet at Utica, St. Leger fled. The Indians were weary; they had lost goods by Willett's sortie; they saw no chance for spoils. Their chiefs killed at Oriskany beckoned them away. They began to abandon the ground, and to spoil the camp of their allies. St.

47. Letter of Schuyler in *Annals of Tryon County*.
48. Manuscript Letter in the *Clinton Collection*, in State Library at Albany. See Appendix.

Leger deemed his danger from them, if he refused to follow their councils, greater than from the enemy. He hurried his wounded and prisoners forward; he left his tents, with most of his artillery and stores, spoils to the garrison.[49] His men threw away their packs in their flight. He quarrelled with Johnson, and the Indians had to make peace between them. St. Leger indeed was helpless. The flight became a disgraceful rout. The Indians butchered alike prisoners and British who could not keep up, or became separated from the column.[50] St. Leger's expedition, as one of the latest became one of the most striking illustrations to the British of the risks and terrors of an Indian alliance.[51]

The siege of Fort Stanwix was raised. The logic of the battle of Oriskany was consummated. The whole story has been much neglected, and the best authorities on the subject are British.[52] The battle is one of a series of events which constitute a chain of history as picturesque, as exciting, as heroic, as important, as ennoble any part of this or any other land.

---

49. Gordon's *History*, vol. 2, who cites Reverend Samuel Kirkland "who was part of the time at the Fort," as his direct informant.
50. *British Annual Register*, for 1777. See Appendix.
51. As a record not familiar to many American readers, see in Appendix, the Narrative of his Expedition by St. Leger himself.
52. For portions of the record. Stone's *Life of Brant* must be excepted as a faithful and accurate chronicle.

2

The Weight and Measure
of the Battle

Oriskany it is our duty to weigh and measure. Wherein was the stand of Greeks at Thermopylae braver, than this march of Herkimer into the ravine? Wherein have Norse Vikings shown sturdier stuff in fight? Tell me when panoplied crusader ever made more light of death than those unmailed farmers of the Mohawk. Cite from verse of ancient or modern poet the *élan* of truer courage, the steadiness of sterner determination, the consecration of more glowing patriotism than held the pass at Oriskany.

THE STRATEGY HISTORIC.

The strategy of the British campaign of 1777 was comprehensive, and it was traditional. With Canada hostile to the country south of it, the plan of Burgoyne was as natural as it is for a pugilist to strike with both fists. Fronting southward, indeed, the blow by Lake Champlain the Canadian forces deliver with their left fist; the route by Lake Ontario through Oswego inland, invites the blow of the right hand. As early as 1687 the French government received from Canada a memorial which recommends:

The Iroquois must be attacked in two directions. The first, and principal attack must be on the Seneca nation, on the borders of Lake Ontario; the second, by the river Richelieu

32

and Lake Champlain, in the direction of the Mohawks.[1]

The French authorities never abandoned this purpose until they were driven from the continent. Frontenac wrote his name in fire and blood in the way Burgoyne sought to travel. The co-operation of the fleet at the mouth of the Hudson, was proposed by Mons. Callierres in 1689.[2] Montcalm [3] led the French by these paths in 1756, when DeLery penetrated to Fort Bull, at the carry near the Mohawk, and the English power yielded up Champlain and Lake George to the invaders. Holding the southern shores of Lake Ontario, it was from Lake Champlain, with co-operation by a force brought up the St. Lawrence, that the English dealt the return attack in 1759, when Wolfe fell before Quebec. At Ticonderoga and Crown Point, on the path to the Hudson, and at Niagara on Lake Ontario, the French power in America breathed its last.

In October, 1776, Sir Guy Carleton had swept over Lake Champlain, and taken Crown Point, and only waited for another season to carry his conquests southward. It was, perhaps, because in London Burgoyne criticised the neglect to send a corps by way of Oswego, through the Mohawk valley, to assist in the campaign, that he, instead of Carleton, led the invasion which ended so disastrously for Britain.

But the British government had earlier precedents than these for choosing these routes for the campaign of 1777. The French migration came by them into the wilderness which is now New York, and it was by them that, at intervals for a hundred years the Iroquois and their allies carried terror to the walls of Montreal and Quebec.[4] The campaigns of the war of 1812 renewed the

---

1. Paris Documents.
2. *Ibid*.
3. See the *Memoir of the French War of 1755-60*, by M. Pouchot, translated by F. B. Hough. M. Pouchot, who was with Montcalm, could learn of no routes from Canada to the English possessions except, 1, by way of Lake Champlain; 2, by the St. Lawrence to Oswego and the Oswego river; 3, by Lake Ontario to the Genesee River; and 4, by way of Niagara to the Ohio River.
4. The Mohawks and Oneidas appeared before Montreal, August 12, 1602; Brodhead's *History of New York*, vol. 1, p. 705. The Iroquois in 1688; vol. 2.

traditions of the military importance of the line of Lake Ontario and Lake Champlain. Oswego and Plattsburg and McDonough's victory perpetuate the series of contests in this historic field. The key to the heart of the original Union lies in the heights from which flow the Mohawk and the Hudson.

St. Leger's Expedition a Vital Part.

In the original plan, St. Leger's expedition is stated as a "diversion," both by Burgoyne and in the official letter of Lord George Germaine, the secretary of state for war. The command was given to St. Leger from Whitehall, on Burgoyne's nomination, so that it was an independent expedition. The troops were in like manner selected, because much depended on the movement. Upon his success, as it proved, the campaign hung. When Burgoyne explained his failure, he laid much stress on the defeat of St. Leger,' and one of the chief points to account for his own slowness, is; "the time entitled me to expect Lieutenant Colonel St. Leger's corps would be arrived at Ticonderoga, and secret means had been long concerted to enable him to make an effort to join me, with probability of success."

And because St. Leger "had been obliged to retreat," he assigns as removing "the first plausible motive in favour of hazardous battle," when he was near Saratoga. In the campaign of 1777, the expedition to the Mohawk was one of the two wings without which success was impossible, which once clipped, crippled everything. The Battle of Bennington was brought on by a British movement having two objects in view, first, to obtain supplies, and second, to create a diversion to aid St. Leger.[5] Every historian who writes of Burgoyne's operations, treats the expedition to the Mohawk as in a military sense a vital element in them. [6]

---

5. Stedman's *History of the Revolution*, (one of the best British records of the struggle;) *Bancroft*, vol. 5.

6. See Appendix, for authorities. Burgoyne himself in urging considerations justifying his advance, in a letter to Lord Germaine, says, (*Defence*, Appendix:) "Colonel St. Leger's operations would have been assisted, a junction with him probably secured, and the whole country to the Mohawk opened."

EFFECT OF ORISKANY ON THE VALLEY AND THE INDIANS.

But we get a faint view of the purpose of the expedition, and of the significance of Oriskany, if we look only at military considerations. Its moral influence was great and far-reaching. Sir John Johnson boasted that the Tories were as five to one in the Mohawk valley, and when he came at the head of a British army, they would rise for the king. Through Johnson and Brant, the design was fostered of holding the Six Nations closely to the royal cause, and thus crushing out the whole patriot influence west of the Hudson. Both purposes were shrewd, and had fair grounds. The patriots knew of these dangers.

In the summons which had aroused Tryon County, they had been told: "one resolute blow would secure the friendship of the Six Nations." The committee of Safety knew the efforts it cost to maintain the authority of Congress. Herkimer fought at Oriskany against a Tory rising at Johnstown, against the complete enlistment of the Iroquois with the British. His victory is measured only when we remember that no Tory rising ever disgraced the Mohawk valley, and that from that hour the Indians were a source of terror and of weakness to the forces of King George.

EFFECT ON THE COUNTRY.

The effect of Oriskany, on the Americans, was electric. Washington said "Herkimer first reversed the gloomy scene" of the campaign. General Gates wrote of "the severe blow General Herkimer gave Johnson and the scalpers under his command."

General Schuyler in replying to General Herkimer's report, said:

> The gallantry of you and the few men that stood with you and repulsed such a superior number of savages, reflects great honour upon you.

Governor George Clinton expressed:

> . . . .the highest sense of the loyalty, valour and bravery of the militia of Tryon County, manifested in the victory

gained by them under the command of their late worthy General Herkimer, for which as the chief magistrate of the free and independent State of New York, they have my most hearty thanks.[7]

The defence of Fort Stanwix led John Adams to declare that "Gansevoort has proved that it is possible to hold a post," and the Oneida Spencer had warned the Tryon patriots not to make a Ticonderoga of Fort Stanwix.

These wise leaders estimated the battle better than writers like Irving,[8] who intimates that "it does not appear that either party was entitled to the victory," or Doctor Thacher,[9] who can only claim that "St. Leger's victory over our militia was purchased at a dear price," or Lossing[10] who bluntly speaks of "the defeat of Herkimer." The patriots held the ground, and carried off their wounded at leisure. Of the Tory wounded Major Watts lay two days uncared for. By the battle St. Leger was bottled up in his camp; by it, the forces ordered with Arnold, and probably also, the Massachusetts troops who took part in Willett's sortie, were able to join in the operations against Burgoyne and were in the first battle of Stillwater.[11] The whole valley of the Mohawk cast itself into the scales for the victory of Saratoga.[12]

Herkimer started for Fort Stanwix, and his force except a few scouts did not reach it. His little army was broken up. But its sacrifice, costly as it was, saved the valley. The frightful slaughter of their leaders at first paralyzed the settlers, but they rallied without delay and joined Arnold's relief army in large numbers.[13] The battle penned St. Leger and Johnson and Brant before Fort Stanwix. It raised the spirits of the beleaguered garrison

---

7. See Appendix for the letter copied from the original manuscript at Albany.
8. *Life of Washington*, vol. 3.
9. *Military Journal*.
10. *Pictoral Field-Book of the Revolution*, vol. 1.
11. Lossing's *Field-Book*, vol. 1, enumerates at Stillwater, all the regiments which marched up the valley with Arnold, and Colonel Wesson's Massachusetts regiment, of which was the detachment which reached Fort Stanwix on the second of August.
12. See Appendix for testimony from leading British, authorities, as well as others.
13. Arnold's letter to Colonel Gansevoort, August 22, 1877.

to a high pitch.[14] With Bennington which came afterwards, the Americans felt it gave them "great and glorious victories,"[15] and "nothing exceeded their exultation" over them; and the "northern militia began now to look high, and to forget all distinctions between themselves and regular troops."

This confidence was worth armies. Congress voted a monument to Herkimer, not yet erected save in the hearts of the people, and no one questioned that the gallant chief had earned the distinction. To Colonel Willett a sword was presented by Congress for his noble exploit, and Colonel Gansevoort received the thanks of Congress, a colonel's commission, and a special designation as commandant of the Fort which he had so bravely defended.

Aims and Estimates on Both Sides.

The Battle of Oriskany and the defence of Fort Stanwix are Siamese twins. Separate events, they are so conjoined that they must be treated as inseparable in fact. The battle so paralyzed St. Leger and demoralized his army, that the siege became a failure. It is notable that British historians nearest to the event, give to Oriskany a degree of prominence which our own writers have hardly equalled. The defeat of St. Leger's expedition British writers of that day, recognize as one of the pivots on which Saratoga was lost and won, and British sentiment agrees that "Saratoga was indeed the turning point of the American struggle."[16]

The *British Annual Register*, noteworthy because established by Edmund Burke, and because its historical articles were still revised if not written by him, in the volume for 1777, published the next year, clearly indicates that the valley of the Mohawk was the very eye of the campaign. [17] This judgment is the more important because the identical text is embodied in the *History of the War* printed in Dublin, 1779, and has become standard in England. In the *Impartial History*, after Burgoyne's arrival at Ticonderoga, the author says:

14. See Appendix for Governor Clinton's letter to Committee of Safety, August 22nd, in New York State Library.
15. *British Annual Register*, 1777; see Appendix.

It is not to be wondered at, if both officers and private men (in Burgoyne's army) were highly elated with their fortune, and deemed that and their prowess to be irresistible; if they regarded their enemy with the greatest contempt, and considered their own toils to be nearly at an end; Albany to be already in their hands, and the reduction of the northern provinces to be rather a matter of some time, than an arduous task full of difficulty and danger.[18]

Erroneously referring to Bennington, the same author uses words justly applicable to Oriskany:[19]

This was the first instance in the present campaign, in which fortune seemed even wavering, much less that she for a moment quitted the royal standard. The exultation was accordingly great on the one side; nor could the other avoid feeling some damp to that eagerness of hope, and receiving some cheek to that assured confidence of success, which an unmixed series of fortunate events must naturally excite.

The shield had been fully reversed, within a single month.

St. Leger claimed that Johnson won "the completest victory," but this was on the assumption "that the militia would never rally." [20] He miscalculated the blow; it was not fatal to the patriots; its consequences were fatal to his plans. The check which he received at Oriskany and his consequent delay, forced Burgoyne to take the risk which brought on him the defeat at Bennington. Although second in importance as well as in older of time, Stedman,[21] one of the best British authorities, names the Vermont fight first in order, as does the *British Impartial History*, (London, 1780,) fixing Bennington properly on August 16th, but for the affair on the Mohawk, naming no date until St.

---

16. *English Cyclopedia*, article on Burgoyne.
17. See Appendix for the words of the Register.
18. *Impartial History of the War in America*, London, 1780.
19. *Ibid.*
20. Letter to Burgoyne, August 11, 1777. *Remembrancer*, 1777. See Appendix.
21. See Appendix for the citation.

Leger's flight on the twenty-second of August.

The *History of the War* published in Dublin, 1779, places the Battle of Oriskany on the sixteenth of August, on the same day as that of Bennington. In spite of this reversal of the order of time, all these authorities concede to the affair at Oriskany, a measure of importance which the occupants of the historic field only begin to assert. As the first blow of the campaign, Oriskany has to the campaign of 1777, the primacy which Lexington has to the whole war.

The failure of St. Leger cut off the right arm of Burgoyne. Burgoyne still clinging to his hopes, believed if Sir Henry Clinton had reached the Highlands earlier, as he did when too late, he "should have had his way."[22] But his own detailed statement proves that he felt that the grave of his campaign was dug when a loyalist rising was prevented in the Mohawk valley;[23] and that was the achievement of Herkimer and the heroes of Oriskany.

The success of St. Leger at Oriskany and Fort Stanwix would have been fatal. The Mohawk valley would have been overrun by the Tories. Albany would have fallen, and Gates been overpowered. Defeat, decided and prompt, would have turned St. Leger back to Oswego, and enabled him with the remnant of his corps, to open a retreat for Burgoyne .as the latter intimates had been contingently concerted.[24] For the emergency of a defeat which closed the Mohawk valley, and of a siege which held him for three weeks before Fort Stanwix, no calculation had been made. It was this combination which proved so fortunate for the republic.

Divisions in the Valley: Dangers Averted.

The dangers to the American cause in the valley, were peculiar. To the German settlers King George had always been a foreign king. They owed him neither affection nor allegiance. It was easy for them to sustain Congress and to fight for independence.

---

22. *Defence.*
23. See Appendix for his own words.
24. Burgoyne's *Defence*, (London, 1780).

They had been jealous of the influence of the Johnsons over the Indians, and over the valley, and that pique was fully reciprocated. Besides the ties of family favour and apparent interest, the Johnsons clung all the more closely to the royal cause, because the Germans took the other part. Something of religious feeling entered into the division, for the Johnsons stood for the Church of England, and Kirkland and other dissenting ministers had been pressing for independence in faith and practice.[25] The interior of New York had felt little or nothing of the burden of taxes which had stirred the other colonies. No royal charter had ever been in force over the State.

The settlers who came from Britain hither lacked the causes for separation which stirred New England and the South, and when the immigrants from other lands enlisted for Congress, the Tory leaders confidently trusted that they could carry the British colonists for King George. Many causes prevented. The patriot leaders were shrewd and diligent, and they were on the soil, while the Tory chiefs were absent. For no long time is it possible that New York shall be alien from New England and the States on our southern borders. But the fight at Oriskany came at the right time to kindle the patriot fires, to draw the lines between the belligerents, to merge old world antagonisms into American patriotism. In the blood shed in that historic field, New York was baptized as a State, and as a State in an enduring republic, in a united nation.

SIGNIFICANCE FROM LOCATION.

The Battle of Oriskany was the more significant because it was fought near the centre of the Long House of the Iroquois. Indian phrase had so styled the valley, for which they placed the western door at the opening of the waters at Niagara, and the eastern door where the Mohawk seeks the Hudson.[26] It was held with its approaches, when the white men came, by the Six Nations, the master tribes among the Indians. They had discovered its fitness for the path of empire and the seat of dominion.

---

25. See Lothrop's *Life of Rev. Samuel Kirkland* for a notable illustration.
26. Morgan's *League of the Iroquois*.

Cadwallader Colden, in 1738, in an official report,[27] noted the peculiar feature that here "some branches of the largest rivers of North America, and which run contrary courses, take their rise within two or three miles of each other;" the Mohawk flowing into the Hudson, the St. Lawrence finding affluents to carry northward, the Susquehanna to add to Chesapeake bay; and from the western walls of the Long House, waters seek the Mississippi and the Gulf.

This configuration gave, naturally, political and military significance to what is now the centre of New York.[28] The Iroquois from it became little less than lords of the continent. Into it the French missionaries early came to spy out the land, with that devotion which led Father Jogues[29] to "write the name of Jesus on the barks of trees in the Mohawk Valley," in 1642, and that foresight which for generations prompted the French Governors of Canada to aim to expel the English by the instrumentality of the Iroquois.[30] In critical periods the British found the Iroquois, by their fidelity and prowess, a sufficient bulwark against French encroachments.[31] From Manhattan the Dutch had reached out, and planted Fort Orange at Albany, and had made friends and kept friends with the Iroquois.

Over from the New England settlements the English crowded into lands whose advantages they clearly saw, and the English Governors at Manhattan were glad to frame treaties to grant to the Iroquois the same advantages which they had enjoyed from the Dutch.[32] Yet the first permanent settlers in a portion of the valley were Germans from the palatinate, who came hither in 1712-13, after stopping on the Hudson.[33] Sir William Johnson,

27. Documentary *History of New York*, vol. 4.
28. DeWitt Clinton's *Address on the Iroquois*. Campbell's *Life of Clinton*. Brodhead's *History of New York*, vol. 2.
29. *Bancroft*, vol. 2.
30. Paris Documents, *Documentary History*, vol. 9.
31. *Bancroft*, vol. 2.
32. Brodhead's *History of New York*, vol. 1.
33. Certain Germans who had sought England for a refuge, it is said, became interested in the Mohawks who visited Queen Anne, and were by the chiefs induced to migrate to America.

himself an Irishman, took great pains to gather British colonists about him, and was in large measure successful, and the Scotch colony was influential and self-asserting. As from the Long House of the Iroquois, waters flow in all directions, so into it tended currents of population from all directions. The Dutch proprietors could not stop this cosmopolitan drift. The German immigration prevented tendencies so distinctively British as prevailed in other colonies. The large share of northern New York in the Anglo-French wars, continued its traditional importance. [34]

Here between Ontario and Champlain, it was decided that the nascent State should be cosmopolitan and not Dutch.[35] Here in large part it was decided, if not that the political relations of the State should be British and not French, that the language, the civilization, the social tendencies should be cast in the mould of Hampden and Milton and Shakespeare, rather than in those of Paris and Versailles. This whole region had indeed been included in New France. Louis XVI and his ministers watched events here with especial interest, and naturally desired that Britain should not continue to possess what France had lost. If St. Leger was beaten where Frontenac and Montcalm had swept in victory, the infant republic, with French aid, might stand and grow a rival to British power. Here large impetus was given to the decision that this continent should be American and not British.

The location of Oriskany rendered the battle controlling in determining the attitude of the Mohawk valley, and in putting an end to British hopes of loyalist uprising there. It shattered and rendered useless the British alliance with the Indians. It helped to insure French co-operation with the colonies, and brought us the fleet of D'Estaing the next summer. It paved the way to

---

34. Ex-Governor Horatio Seymour, in his lecture on the *History and Topography of New York*, has admirably presented the relations of the State, growing out of its natural situation.

35. August 1, 1802, Rev. John Taylor, a missionary from New England, visited Utica on his way west, and says of it: "Utica appears to be a mixed mass of discordant materials. Here may be found people of ten or twelve different nations, and of almost all religions and sects."

the victory over Burgoyne. Without Oriskany, there could have been no Saratoga. Herkimer laid in blood the corner-stone of that temple of unwinged victory, which was completed on the heights where Burgoyne surrendered. Afterwards through the long contest, although local raids and savage butcheries were perpetrated, no operations of grand war were attempted in these historic regions. While nominally British purposes were unchanged, the colonies north and east of New York bay escaped the ravages of broad conflict, and entered upon their career of national growth and prosperity.

CONCLUSION.

Extravagant eulogy never honours its object. Persistent neglect of events which have moulded history, is not creditable to those who inherit the golden fruits. We do not blush to grow warm over the courage which at Plataea saved Greece forever from Persian invasion. Calm men praise the determination which at Lepanto, set limits to Turkish conquests in Europe. Waterloo is the favourite of rhetoric among English-speaking people. But history no less exalts the Spartan three hundred who died at Thermopylae, and poetry immortalizes the six hundred whose leader blundered at Balaklava. Signally negligent have the people of Central New York been to the men and the deeds that on the soil we daily tread, have controlled the tides of nations, and fashioned the channels of civilization.

After a hundred years, (at time of first publication), we begin to know what the invasion of St. Leger meant. A century lifts up Nicholas Herkimer, if not into a consummate general, to the plane of sturdy manliness and of unselfish, devoted patriotism, of a hero who knew how to fight and how to die. History begins to appreciate the difficulties which surrounded Philip Schuyler, and to see that he appeared slow in bringing out the strength of a patriot State, because the scales of destiny were weighted to hand New York over to Johnson and Burgoyne and Clinton and King George. His eulogy is, that when popular impatience, and jealousies in other colonies, and ambitious in the army, and cliques in Congress, superseded him in the command of the northern armies of the United States, he had already stirred up the Mohawk valley to the war blaze at Oriskany; he had relieved Fort Stanwix and sent St. Lester in disgraceful retreat; Bennington had been fought and won;[36] he had thus shattered the British alliance with the Indians, and had trampled out the Tory embers in the Mohawk valley; he had gathered above Albany an army flushed with victory and greatly superior to Burgoyne's forces in numbers, and it was well led and adequate to the task before it.

Oriskany, the Indians interpret, is the Place of Nettles. Out of that nettle danger, Herkimer plucked for the Mohawk valley, and through it for the republic, the flower safety. In that Place of Nettles, Central New York may find much to stir it to deeper knowledge of its history and its relations, to greater anxiety to be just to those who have served it worthily, to keener appreciation of the continental elevation which nature has reared for us, and upon which we may build a structure more symmetrical and more beneficent than the Parthenon,—a free State based on equal justice, strong in the virtue of its citizens, devoted to all that is best and most beautiful in mankind, inspired by the noblest achievements in history, manfully meeting the humblest duties, and struggling upward to the highest ideals.

Names and deeds that live a hundred years, change hills and valleys into classic ground. The century which runs backward is only the dawn of those which look into the future. Central New York must have a worthy career before it to justify the traditions of the Long House of the Iroquois; of the real statesmanship of the League of the Six Nations, and of the eloquence of their chief men; of the Jesuit missionaries and the Samuel Kirklands and the Lutheran clergymen, who consecrated its waters and its soil and its trees; of those who saved it from French occupation; of those who kept out the Stuarts and drove out King George.

---

36. General Gates took command of the army before Burgoyne, August 14, 1777, but had nothing to do with Bennington.

Appendix

1. THE NAME ORISKANY.

The orthography of Oriskany has been settled by custom contrary to Indian euphony. St. Leger writes it Oriska; Colonel Willett changes the initial to Eriska; Captain Deygart (Clinton manuscripts) writes Orisco. In London documents, (*Colonial History*, vol. 8,) we find Oriske.

In a *Chorographical map of the Province of New York*, London, 1779, is Ochriscany Patent granted to T. Wenham & Co. In a map of 1790, this becomes Ochriskeney (*Documentary History of New York*, volume 1.)

In his *League of the Iroquois*, L. H. Morgan gives the Indian derivation, showing that the name comes from the Mohawk dialect, and the last syllable is a corruption. In the several dialects the form is as follows:

Seneca dialect, *O-his-heh*;
Cayuga, *O-his-ha*;
Onondaga, *O-his-ka*;
Tuscarora, *Ose-hase-keh*;
Oneida, *Ole-hisk*;
Mohawk, *Ole-his-ka*;

The significance in each case being the Place of Nettles.

2. BUILDING OF FORT STANWIX.

The building of Fort Stanwix in 1758 is recorded in *Documentary History of New York*, vol. 4, and a topographical map is given of the country between the Mohawk and Wood Creek, from an actual survey in November, 1758. General Abercrombie's order to General Stanwix to erect the fort is there preserved. Fort Williams had at an earlier day stood in the neighbourhood. Fort Stanwix was not finished in 1700, when M. Pouchot passed it. (*Hough's Translation of his Memoir.*)

Out of compliment to General Philip Schuyler the attempt was made to change the name of this fort, but old Peter Schuyler had given the title to the old Fort at Utica, and Stanwix has clung to the historic work at Rome.

3. PEACE COUNCILS AT FORT STANWIX.

In 1768 it had been the scene of an important council, when thirty-two hundred Indians of the Six Nations assembled to treat with representatives of Virginia, Pennsylvania and New Jersey. Sir William Johnson then closed the *Treaty of Fort Stanwix*. The original record will be found in the Documents relating to the *Colonial History of New York*, vol. 8.

In 1784 a grand council was held here between the chiefs of the Six Nations and Commissioners on the part of the United States, and a treaty of peace was negotiated.

4. ST. LEGER'S TROOPS DESIGNATED IN LONDON.

This extract from an official letter from Lord George Germaine to General Carleton, dated Whitehall, twenty-sixth March, 1777, is taken from the *State of the Expedition from Canada*, published in London, 1780, by General Burgoyne in his own defence:

> With a view of quelling the rebellion as quickly as possible, it is become highly necessary that the most speedy junction of the two armies should be effected, and therefore, as the security and good government of Canada absolutely require your presence there, it is the King's determination to leave about 3,000 men under your command, and to employ the remainder of your army upon two expeditions, the one under the command of Lieutenant General Burgoyne, who is to force his way to Albany, and the other under command of Lieutenant Colonel St. Leger, who is

to make a diversion on the Mohawk River.

As this plan cannot be advantageously executed without the assistance of Canadians and Indians, His Majesty strongly recommends it to your care to furnish both expeditions with good and sufficient bodies of those men; and I am happy in knowing that your influence among them is so great that there can be no room to apprehend that you will find it difficult to fulfil His Majesty's expectations.

It is the King's further pleasure that you put under the command of Colonel St. Leger:

Detachment from the 8th Regiment	100
Detachment from the 34th Regiment	100
Sir John Johnson's regiment of New York	133
Hanan Chasseurs	342
	————
	675

together with a sufficient number of Indians and Canadians, and after having furnished him with proper artillery, stores, provisions and every other necessary article for his expedition, and secured to him every assistance in your power to afford and procure, you are to give him orders to proceed forthwith to and down to the Mohawk River to Albany and put himself under the command of Sir William Howe.

I shall write to Sir William Howe from hence by the first packet; but you will nevertheless endeavour to give him the earliest intelligence of this measure, and also direct Lieutenant General Burgoyne and Lieutenant Colonel St. Leger to neglect no opportunity of doing the same, that they may receive instructions from Sir William Howe. You will at the same time inform them that, until they shall have received orders from Sir William Howe, it is His Majesty's pleasure that they act as exigencies may require, and in such manner as they shall judge most proper for making an impression on the rebels and bringing them to obedience; but that in so doing they must never lose, view of their intended junctions with Sir William Howe as their principal, objects.

In case Lieutenant General Burgoyne or Lieutenant Colonel St. Leger should happen to die or be rendered, through illness, incapable of executing these great trusts, you are to nominate to their respective commands such officer or officers as you shall think best qualified to supply the place of those whom His Majesty has, in his wisdom, at present appointed to conduct these expeditions.

5. KIRKLAND AND THE INDIANS.

Reverend Samuel Kirkland wrote to the committee at Albany, June 9, 1775:

> Colonel Johnson has orders from government (of course the British government) to remove the dissenting minister from the Six Nations till the difficulties between Great Britain and the colonies are settled. . . . All he has against me I suppose to be this: A suspicion that I have interpreted to the Indians the doings of the Continental Congress, which has undeceived and too much opened the eyes of the Indians for Colonel Johnson's purposes. I confess to you, gentlemen, that I have been guilty of this, if it be any transgression. . . . . I apprehend my interpreting the doings of the Congress to their *sachems* has done more real service to the cause of the country, or the cause of truth and justice, than £500 in presents would have effected.

Jones' *Annals of Oneida County*.

6. GENERAL SCHUYLER'S FEAR.

In a letter to the Committee of Safety, dated July 24, 1777, General Schuyler says:

> If Burgoyne can penetrate to Albany, the force which is certainly coming by way of Oswego, will find no difficulty in reaching the Mohawk River, and being arrived there

they will be joined by Tories not only, but by every person that finds himself capable of removing, and wishes to make his peace with the enemy, and by the whole body of the Six Nations.

7. SIR JOHN JOHNSON THE BRITISH LEADER AT ORISKANY.

William L. Stone, to whom so much is due for a fair statement of the Battle of Oriskany, insists that Sir John Johnson was not in the battle at all, naming Watts, Butler and Brant, in this order, as leaders. And W. W. Campbell, in his Annals of Tryon county, places the "Indians and Tories under Brant and Butler." Irving in his *Life of Washington* follows these authorities. Stone justifies his denial of Johnson's presence in the battle by Colonel Willett's assertion in his narrative, that Singleton, one of the prisoners taken in the sortie, told him that "Sir John Johnson was with him (Singleton) when the camp was attacked." These words of Willett are in the paraphrase by Willett's son, (*Narrative*) transformed into a statement that Johnson was "in his tent with his coat off, and had not time to put it on before his camp was forced."

In view of the importance of the operations in progress, this statement is intrinsically improbable. It is contradicted by the positive language of St. Leger, who, in his Narrative (Burgoyne's *Defence*) clearly says: "Sir John Johnson put himself at the head of the party," which went to Oriskany, "and began his march that evening at five o'clock, and met the rebel corps at the same hour the next morning." St. Leger attempted a movement against the sortie, but he used Lieutenants only as he could not have done if Johnson had been in camp. See the tenth section of this Appendix.

In an official letter from Colonel Daniel Claus, (St. Leger's superintendent of Indians.) he distinctly avers:

Sir John Johnson asked leave to join his company of light infantry and head the whole, which was granted; Colonel Butler and other Indian officers were ordered with the Indians. *Colonial History*, vol. 8.

President Dwight (*Travels*, vol. 3) who made the battle a study in 1799, at Whitestown and Rome, says: "Sir John had scarcely left the ground to attack General Herkimer." And again after the battle: "At the return of Sir John." This was the clear understanding of the generation to whom about the battlefield and the fort, the fight was as the alphabet; and it has the weight of authority in its favour.

Indeed, taking the language of St. Leger and Claus together, it is absolutely incontrovertible.

8. GENERAL PUTNAM AIDS IN THE RELIEF.

In the *Clinton Papers* at Albany is the original of the following letter:

> Peck's Kill, August 14, 1777.
>
> Dear Sir:—Received yours of the fourteenth inst. In consequence of it and former orders received from General Washington have ordered Colonel Cortlandt's and Colonel Livingston's regiments to march immediately to the northward to the relief of Fort Schuyler, or as you shall see fit to direct them.
>
> I wish them a speedy and safe arrival and you most successful enterprise against those worse than infernals.
>
> With great respect, I am your obedient humble servant,
>
> Israel Putnam.
>
> To his Excellency, Governor Clinton.

9. GOVERNOR CLINTON TO THE COMMITTEE OF SAFETY.

The following is the text of a letter from Governor George Clinton, copied from the original in the State Library at Albany:

> Albany, August 22, 1777.
>
> General Harchheimer is dead of his wounds. His leg was taken off and he survived it but a few hours. General Arnold with his party is at Fort Dayton. About 100 of the militia of Tryon county only are with him. I have issued my positive orders to the officers commanding the re-

spective regiments there to detach one-half to join General Arnold's army. Colonels Cortland's and Livingston's regiments marched this evening for his further reinforcement.

The enemy in that quarter having acquired a considerable accession of numbers from Indians and Tories, the above measures were rendered necessary. The garrison, however, by very late accounts, are high in spirits and well provided, and I have no doubt we shall in a few days receive the most agreeable intelligence from that quarter. From the Oneidas and Tuscaroras, whose chieftains are now with General Arnold, we have the fullest assurance of assistance but have nothing to expect from any other tribes of the Six Nations until our successes intimidate them into friendship. Since the affair at Bennington the scalping business seems to have ceased.

10. St. Leger's Own Narrative.

General Burgoyne published in London, in 1780, a defence of his campaign in America, under the title: *A State of the Expedition from Canada*, as *laid before the House of Commons*. In the Appendix is the following interesting document:

Colonel St. Leger's Account of Occurrences at Fort Stanwix.

A minute detail of every operation since my leaving La Chine, with the detachment entrusted to my care, your Excellency will permit me to reserve to a time of less hurry and mortification than the present, while I enter into the interesting scene before Fort Stanwix, which I invested the third of August, having previously pushed forward Lieutenant Bird of the King's regiment, with thirty of the King's troops and two hundred Indians, under the direction of Captains Hare and Wilson, and the Chiefs Joseph and Bull, to seize fast hold of the lower landing place, and thereby cut off the enemy's communication with the lower country. This was done with great address by the lieutenant, though not attended with the effect I had promised myself occasioned by the slackness of the Messasagoes. The brigade of provisions and ammunition boats I had intelligence of, being arrived and disembarked before this party had taken post.

The fourth and fifth were employed in making arrangements for opening Wood Creek, (which the enemy, with the indefatigable labour of one hundred and fifty men, for fourteen days, had most effectually choaked up,) and the making a temporary road from Pine Ridges, upon Fish Creek, sixteen miles from the fort, for a present supply of provision and the transport of our artillery; the first was effected by the diligence and zeal of Captain Bouville, assisted by Captain Harkimer, of the Indian department, with one hundred and ten men, in nine days; while Lieutenant Lundy, acting as assistant quarter-master general, had rendered the road in the worst of weather, sufficiently practicable to pass the whole artillery and stores, with seven days' provision, in two days.

On the fifth, in the evening, intelligence arrived by my discovering parties on the Mohawk River, that a reinforcement of eight hundred militia, conducted by General Herkimer, were on their march to relieve the garrison, and were actually at that instant at Oriska, an Indian settlement, twelve miles from the fort. The garrison being apprised of their march by four men, who were seen to enter the fort in the morning, through what was thought an impenetrable swamp, I did not think it prudent to wait for them, and thereby subject myself to be attacked by a sally from the garrison in the rear, while the reinforcement employed me in front.

I therefore determined to attack them on the march, either openly or covertly, as circumstances should offer. At this time, I had not two hundred and fifty of the King's troops in camp; the various and extensive operations I was under an absolute necessity of entering into, having employed the rest; and therefore could not send above eighty white men, rangers and troops included, with the whole corps of Indians. Sir John Johnson put himself at the head of this party, and began his march that evening at five o'clock, and met the rebel corps at the same hour the next morning.

The impetuosity of the Indians is not to be described on the sight of the enemy (forgetting the judicious disposition formed by Sir John, and agreed to by themselves, which was to suffer the attack to begin with the troops in front, while they should be on both flanks and rear,) they rushed in, hatchet in hand, and thereby gave the enemy's rear an opportunity to escape. In relation to the victory, it was equally complete, as if the whole had fallen; nay, more so, as the two hundred who escaped only served to spread the panic wider; but it was not so with the Indians; their loss was great, (I must be understood Indian computation, being only about thirty killed and the like number wounded, and in that number some of their favourite chiefs and confidential warriors were slain.)

On the enemy's side, almost all their principal leaders were slain. General Herkimer has since died of his wounds. It is proper to mention, that the four men detached with intelligence of the march of the reinforcement, set out the evening before the action, and consequently the enemy could have no account of the defeat, and were in possession only of the time appointed for their arrival; at which, as I suspected, they made a sally with two hundred and fifty men toward Lieutenant Bird's post, to facilitate the entrance of the relieving corps, or bring on a general engagement, with every advantage they could wish.

Captain Hoyes was immediately detached to cut in upon their rear, while they engaged the lieutenant. Immediately upon the departure of Captain Hoyes, having learned that Lieutenant Bird, misled by the information of a cowardly Indian, that Sir John was pressed, had quitted his post to march to his assistance, I marched the detachment of the King's regiment, in support of Captain Hoyes, by a road in sight of the garrison, which, with executive fire from his party, immediately drove the enemy into the fort, without any further advantage than frightening some squaws and pilfering the packs of the warriors which they left behind them. After this affair was over, orders were immediately given to complete a two-gun battery, and mortar beds, with three strong redoubts in their rear, to enable me, in case of another attempt, to relieve the garrison by their regimented troops, to march out a larger body of the King's troops.

Captain Lernoult was sent with one hundred and ten men to the lower landing place, where he established himself with great judgment and strength, having an enclosed battery of a three-pounder opposed to any sally from the fort, and another to the side of the country, where a relief must approach; and the body of his camp deeply entrenched and abbatised.

When by the unabating labour of officers and men, (the smallness of our numbers never admitting of a relief, or above three hours' cessation for sleep or cooking,) the batteries and redoubts were finished, and new cheeks and axle-trees made for the six-pounders, those that were sent being reported rotten and unserviceable.

It was found that our cannon had not the least effect upon the sod-work of the fort, and that our royals had only the power of teasing, as a six-inch plank was a sufficient security for their powder magazine, as we learnt from the deserters. At this time Lieutenant Glenie, of the artillery, whom I appointed to act as assistant engineer, proposed a conversion of the royals (if I may use the expression) into howitzers. The ingenuity and feasibility of this measure striking me very strongly, the business was set about immediately, and soon executed, when it was found that nothing prevented their operating with the desired effect but the distance, their chambers being too small to hold a sufficiency of powder. There was nothing now to be done but to approach the town by sap to such a distance that the rampart might be brought within their practice, at the same time all materials were preparing to run a mine under their most formidable bastion.

In the midst of these operations intelligence was brought in by our scouts of a second corps of 1,000 men being on their march. The same zeal no longer animated the Indians; they complained of our thinness of troops and their former losses. I immediately called a council of the chiefs; encouraged them as much as I could; promised to lead them on myself, and bring into the field 300 of the best troops. They listened to this, and promised to follow me, and agreed that I should reconnoitre the ground properest for the field of battle the next morning, accompanied by some of their chief warriors to settle the plan of operations.

When upon the ground appointed for the field of battle, scouts came in with the account of the first number swelled to 2,000; immediately after a third, that General Burgoyne's army was cut to pieces, and that Arnold was advancing by rapid and forced marches with 3,000 men. It was at this moment I began to suspect cowardice in some and treason in others; however, I returned to camp, not without hopes, with the assistance of my gallant coadjutor, Sir John Johnson, and the influence of the superintending colonels, Claus and Butler, of inducing them to meet the enemy.

A council, according to their custom, was called, to know their resolutions, before the breaking up of which I learned that 200 were already decamped. In about an hour they insisted that I should retreat, or they would be obliged to abandon me. I had no other party to take, and a hard party it was to troops who could do nothing without them, to yield to their resolves; and therefore proposed to retire at night, sending on before my sick, wounded, artillery, &c, down the Wood Creek, covering them by our line of march.

This did not fall in with their views, which were no less than treacherously committing ravage upon their friends, as they had lost the opportunity of doing it upon their enemies. To effect this they artfully caused messengers to come in, one after the other, with accounts of the near approaches of the rebels; one and the last affirmed that they were within two miles of Captain Lernoult's post. Not giving entire credit to this, and keeping to my resolution of retiring by night, they grew furious and abandoned; seized upon the officers' liquor and cloaths, in spite of the efforts of their servants, and became more formidable than the enemy we had to expect.

I now thought it time to call in Captain Lernoult's post, retiring with the troops in camp to the ruined fort called William, in the front of the garrison, not only to wait the enemy if they thought proper to sally, but to protect the boats from the fury of the savages, having sent forward Captain Hoyes with his detachment, with one piece of cannon, to the place where Bull Fort stood, to receive the troops who waited the arrival of Captain Lernoult. Most of the boats were escorted that night beyond Canada Creek, where no danger was to be apprehended from the enemy. The creek at this place, bending from the road, has a deep cedar swamp between. Every attention was now turned to the mouth of the creek, which the enemy might have possessed themselves of by a rapid march by the Oneyda Castle.

At this place the whole of the little army arrived by twelve o'clock at night, and took post in such a manner as to have no fears of anything the enemy could do. Here we remained till three o'clock next morning, when the boats which could come up the creek arrived, or rather that the rascally part of all nations of the Indians would suffer to come up; and proceeded across Lake Oneyda to the ruined Fort of Brereton, where I learnt that some boats were still labouring down the creek, after being lightened of the best part of their freight by the Messasagoes. Captain Lernoult proposed, with a boat full of armed men, to repass the lake that night to relieve them from their labour, and supply them with provision. This transaction does as much honour to the humanity as to the gallantry of this valuable officer.

On my arrival at the Onondago Falls I received an answer to my letter from Your Excellency, which showed, in the clearest light, the scenes of treachery that had been practiced upon me. The messenger had heard in deed on his way that they were collecting the same kind of rabble as before, but that there was not an enemy within forty miles of Fort Stanwix.

Soon after my arrival here I was joined by Captain Lernoult, with the men and boats he had been in search of. I mean immediately to send off for the use of the upper garrison, all the overplus provisons I shall have, after keeping a sufficiency to carry my detachment down, which I mean to do with every expedition in my power the moment this business is effected, for which purpose I have ordered here the snow. The sloop is already gone from this with her full lading.

Officers from each corps are sent to Montreal to procure necessaries for the men, who are in a most deplorable situation from the plunder of the savages, that no time may be lost to join your army.

I have the honour to be, with the greatest respect, sir, Your Excellency's most obedient and most faithful servant,

Barry St. Leger.

Oswego, August 27, 1777.
His Excellency General Burgoyne.

11. British Authority on the Importance of St. Leger's Expedition.

The first authority on this point is General Burgoyne, who in his paper "for conducting the war from the side of Canada," urges the expedition by "the Lake Ontario and Oswego to the Mohawk River, which," he says, "as a diversion *to facilitate every proposed operation*, would be highly desirable." (*Defence*, Appendix.)

Second. It will be remarked in the letter of Lord George Germaine, he announces "the King's determination" to employ the army in Canada "upon two expeditions," one by Burgoyne and the other by St. Leger, thus placing both on the same footing. See the extract from the letter in the fourth section of this Appendix.

The third authority to be cited on this point is the *British Annual Register* for 1777, (under the auspices at least of Edmund Burke,) where we read:

> In these embarrassing and difficult circumstances General Burgoyne received information that Colonel St. Leger had arrived before and was conducting his operations against Fort Stanwix. He instantly and justly conceived that a rapid movement forward at this critical period would be of utmost importance. If the enemy proceeded up the Mohawk and that St. Leger succeeded, he would be liable to get between two fires, or at any rate, General Burgoyne's army would get between him and Albany, so that he must either stand an action or by passing the Hudson's River, endeavour to secure a retreat higher up to the New England provinces. If, on the other hand, he abandoned Fort Stanwix to its fate, and fell back to Albany, the Mohawk country would of course be entirely laid open, the juncture with St. Leger established, and the entire army at liberty and leisure to prescribe and choose its future line of operation.

General Burgoyne in his *Defence* uses these words:

It will likewise be remembered that Lieutenant Colonel St. Leger was at this time before Fort Stanwix; every hour was pregnant with critical events.

The History of the Civil War, by an Officer of the (British) Army, London, 1780, says:

Fortune, which had been hitherto favourable to General Burgoyne, now began to withdraw her caresses, and like a flirting female, broke from him in the moment of possession.

Consult also section thirteenth of this Appendix.

12. Governor Clinton on the Battle of Oriskany and the Tryon County Militia.

The following important letter is found in the original manuscript in the State Library at Albany. It was addressed to the several colonels in Tryon County:

Headquarters, Half Moon, 22nd August, 1777.
Sir: While I have the highest sense of the loyalty, valour and bravery of the militia of Tryon County, manifested in the victory gained by them under the command of their late worthy General Herkimer, for which, as the chief magistrate of the free and independent State of New York, they have my most hearty thanks, it gives me the greatest pain to be informed that any difficulty should arise in their joining the army under General Arnold, and thereby enabling him to finish the war in that quarter by raising the siege of Fort Schuyler and destroying the enemy's army in that quarter, and restoring peace and safety to the inhabitants of Tryon County.
Their noble exertions against the common enemy have already gained them the greatest honour, their perseverance will secure them peace and safety. In both I am greatly interested, and it is my duty and I hereby most positively order that you immediately join General Arnold with one-half of your regiment completely armed, equipt and

accoutred, and march under his command to the relief of Fort Schuyler. As soon as the service will admit General Arnold will dismiss you. If any are hardy enough to refuse to obey your orders given in consequence of this, you are immediately to report the names of the same to General Arnold, who will transmit the same to me, that they may be dealt with with the utmost rigor of the law.

I am your obedient servant,

George Clinton.

Frederick Sammons in his manuscript narrative, states that Arnold, after he had relieved the fort, "directly marched his troops to Stillwater." Sammons was in this army. He had been off on duty as a scout in the early days of August.

13. THE MOHAWK VALLEY AT SARATOGA.

The *History of the Civil War in America, by an Officer in the British Army*, Captain Hall, London, 1780, says:

The retreat of Colonel St. Leger inspired the enemy with fresh ardour, and as they had now no longer anything to fear on the Mohawk river, a numerous and hardy militia from that country immediately joined their army in the neighborhood of Albany, which now advanced and took post near Stillwater, where they were also joined by a body of troops under Arnold, who had, in fact, been detached to the relief of Fort Stanwix, though he was at a great distance when the finesse of the garrison succeeded in saving the place.

Botta's History of the United States declares specifically:

The successes of the Americans under the walls of Fort Schuyler, (Stanwix,) besides having inspired the militia, produced also the other happy effect of enabling them, relieved from the fear of invasion in the country upon the Mohawk, to unite all their forces against the army of Burgoyne. (Vol. 1.)

In the *History of the war with America, France and Spain, by John Andrews, LL. D.*, (London, 1786,) vol. 2, the case is thus stated:

The failure of the expedition against Fort Stanwix, together with the defeat of Bennington, were very severe blows to the British interest in those parts. They animated the Americans to a surprising degree. They began now confidently to promise themselves that General Burgoyne himself would share the same fate as his officers.

General Burgoyne in a letter to Lord Germaine, dated Camp, near Saratoga, August 20, 1777, says:

I am afraid the expectations of Sir J. Johnson greatly fail in the rising of the country. On this side I find daily reason to doubt the sincerity of the resolution of the professing loyalists. I have about four hundred, but not half of them armed, who may be depended upon; the rest are trimmers, merely actuated by interest. The great bulk of the country is undoubtedly with the Congress, in principle and zeal; and their measures are executed with a secrecy and dispatch that are not to be equalled.

General Burgoyne, in his *Defence* presents this as a conclusive argument in his own behalf:

The circumstances of the action at Bennington established a yet more melancholy conviction of the fallacy of any dependence upon supposed friends. The noble Lord has said, that. 'I never despaired of the campaign before the affair at Bennington; that I had no doubt of gaining Albany, in as short a time as the army (in due condition of supply) could accomplish the march.' I acknowledge the truth of the assertions in their fullest extent; all my letters at the time show it, I will go further and in one sense apply with the noble lord the epithet 'fatal' to the affair of Bennington. The knowledge I acquired of the professors of loyalty was 'fatal' and put an end to every expectation from enterprise, unsustained by dint of force.

It would have been excess of frenzy to have trusted for sustenance to the plentiful region of Albany. Had the march thither been unopposed, the enemy, finding the British army unsupplied, would only have had to compel the Tories to drive the cattle and destroy the corn, and the capitulation of Albany instead of Saratoga must have followed. Would the Tories have risen? Why did they not rise around Albany and below when they found Mr. Gates' army increasing by separate and distinct parties from remote distances? They were better qualified by their situation to catch the favourable moment, than I was to advise it.

Why did they not rise in that populous, and, as supposed, well affected district, the German Flats, at the time St. Leger was before Fort Stanwix? A critical insurrection from any one point to create diversion would probably have secured the success of the campaign. But to revert to the reasons against a rapid march after the affair of Bennington. It was then also known that by the false intelligence respecting the strength of Fort Stanwix, the infamous behaviour of the Indians and the want of the promised co-operation of the loyal inhabitants, St. Leger had been obliged to retreat. The first plausible motive in favor of hazardous haste, the facilitating his descent of the Mohawk, was at an end.

It is pleasant to add to this testimony the following:

COUNCIL OF SAFETY TO JOHN HANCOCK,
PRESIDENT OF CONGRESS.

Kingston, August 26, 1777.
Sir: I have the pleasure of transmitting to you the letters of General Schuyler and Governor Clinton, giving us the agreeable intelligence of the raising of the siege of Fort Schuyler. The gallantry of the commander of the garrison of that Fort and the distinguished bravery of General Herkimer and his militia, have already been productive of the most desirable consequences. The brave and more for-

tunate General Stark with his spirited countrymen hath, as you know, given the enemy a signal coup at Bennington. The joint result of these providential instances of success hath revived the drooping hopes of the desponding and given new vigour to the firm and determined. We have therefore the pleasing expectation of compelling General Burgoyne in his turn to retire.

I have the honour to be, &c,

Pierre Van Cortlandt.

14. THE BRITISH ACCOUNT OF THE AFFAIR.

The *British Annual Register* for 1777 makes the following statement of the affair, which has become the standard British history:

St. Leger's attempt upon Fort Stanwix (now named by the Americans Fort Schuyler,) was soon after its commencement favoured by a success so signal as would, in other cases and a more fortunate season, have been decisive, as to the fate of a stronger and more important fortress. General Herkimer, a leading man of that country, was marching at the head of eight or nine hundred of the Tryon County militia, with a convoy of provisions, to the relief of the fort. St. Leger, well aware of the danger of being attacked in his trenches, and of withstanding the whole weight of the garrison in some particular and probably weak point at the same instant, judiciously detached Sir John Johnson with some regulars, the whole or part of his own regiment and the savages, to lie in ambush in the wood and interrupt the enemy upon their march.

It should seem by the conduct of the militia and their leader, that they were not only totally ignorant of all military duties, but that they had even never hear! by report of the nature of an Indian war, or of that peculiar service in the woods, to which from its nature and situation this country was at all times liable. Without examination of their ground, without a reconnoitering or flanking party, they plunged blindly into the trap that was laid for their destruction. Being thrown into a sudden and inevitable disorder, by a near and heavy fire on almost all sides, it was completed by the Indians who, instantly pursuing their fire, rushed in upon their broken ranks and made a most dreadful slaughter amongst them with their spears and hatchets.

Notwithstanding their want of conduct the militia shewed no want of courage in their deplorable situation. In the midst of such extreme danger, and so bloody an execution rendered still more terrible by the horrid appearance and demeanour of the principal actors, they recollected themselves so far as to recover an advantageous ground, which enabled them after to maintain a sort of running fight, by which about one-third of their number was preserved.

The loss was supposed to be on their side about four hundred killed, and half that number prisoners. It was thought of the greater consequence, as almost all those who were considered as the principal leaders and instigators of rebellion in that country were now destroyed. The triumph and exultation were accordingly great, and all opposition from the militia in that country was supposed to be at an end. The circumstance of old neighbourhood and personal knowledge between many of the parties, in the present rage and animosity of faction could by no means be favourable to the extension of mercy; even supposing that it might have been otherwise practiced with prudence and safety, at a time when the power of the Indians was rather prevalent, and that their rage was implacable.

For according to their computation and ideas of loss the savages had purchased this victory exceeding dearly, thirty-three of their number having been slain and twenty-nine wounded, among whom were several of their principal leaders and of their most distinguished and favourite warriors. The loss accordingly rendered them so discontented, intractable and ferocious that the service was greatly affected by their ill disposition. The unhappy prisoners were, however, its first objects, most of whom they inhumanly butchered in cold blood. The New Yorkers, Rangers and other troops were not without loss in this action.

On the day, and probably during the time of this engagement, the garrison, having received intelligence of the approach of their friends, endeavoured to make a diversion in their favour by a vigorous and well-conducted sally, under the direction of Colonel Willet, their second in command. Willet conducted his business with ability and spirit. He did considerable mischief in the camp, brought off some trophies, no inconsiderable spoil, some of which consisted in articles that were greatly wanted, a few prisoners, and retired with little or no loss. He afterwards undertook, in company with another officer, a much more perilous expedition. They passed by night through the besiegers' works, and in contempt of the danger and cruelty of the savages, made their way for fifty miles through pathless woods and unexplored morasses, in order to raise the country and bring relief to the fort. Such an action demands the praise even of an enemy.

Colonel St. Leger left no means untried to profit of his victory by intimidating the garrison. He sent verbal and written messages stating their hopeless situation, the utter destruction of their friends, the impossibility of their obtaining relief, as General Burgoyne, after destroying everything in his power, was now at Albany receiving the submission of all the adjoining counties, and by prodigiously magnifying his own force. He represented that in this state of things if through an incorrigible obstinacy, they should continue hopeless and fruitless defence, they would according to the practice of the most civilized nations be cut off from all conditions and every hope of mercy.

But he was particularly direct upon the pains he had taken in softening the rage of the Indians from their late loss and obtaining from them security that in case of an immediate surrender of the fort every man of the garrison should be spared, while on the other hand they declared with utmost bitter execrations that if they met with any further resistance they would not only massacre the garrison, but that every man, woman and child in the Mohawk country would necessarily, and however against his will, fall sacrifices to the fury of the savages.

This point, he said, he pressed entirely on the score of humanity. He promised on his part, in case of an immediate surrender, every attention which a humane and generous enemy could give. The Governor, Colonel Gansevoort, behaved with great firmness. He replied that he had been entrusted with the charge of that garrison by the United States of America; that he would defend the trust committed to his care at every hazard and to the utmost extremity, and that he should not at all concern himself about any consequences that attended the discharge of his duty. It was shrewdly remarked in the fort that half the pains would not have been taken to display the force immediately without or the success at a distance if they bore any proportion at all to the magnitude in which they were represented.

The British commander was much disappointed in the state of the fort It was stronger, in better condition, and much better defended than he expected. After great labour in his approaches he found his artillery deficient, being insufficient in weight to make any considerable impression. The only remedy was to bring his approaches so near that they must take effect, which he set about with the greatest diligence.

In the meantime the Indians continued sullen and untractable. Their late losses might have been cured by certain advantages, but the misfortune was they had yet got no plunder, and their prospect of getting any seemed to grow every day fainter. It is the peculiar characteristic of that people to exhibit in certain instances degrees of courage and perseverance which shock reason and credibility, and to portray in others the greatest irresolution and timidity, with a total want of that constancy which might enable them for any length of time to struggle with difficulty.

Whilst the commander was carrying on his operations with the utmost industry the Indians received a flying report that Arnold was coming with 1,000 men to relieve the fort. The commander endeavoured to hasten them, by promising to lead them himself, to bring all his best troops into action, and by carrying their leaders out to mark a field of battle, and the flattery of consulting them upon the intended plans of operation. Whilst he was thus endeavouring to soothe their temper and to revive their flagging spirits, other scouts arrived with intelligence, probably contrived in part by themselves, which first doubled and afterwards trebled the number of the enemy, with the comfortable addition that Burgoyne's army was entirely cut to pieces.

The Colonel returned to camp, and called a council of their chiefs hoping that by the influence which Sir John Johnson and Superintendents Claus and Butler, had over them, they might still be induced to make a stand. He was disappointed. A part of the Indians decamped whilst the council was sitting and the remainder threatened peremptorily to abandon him if he did not immediately retreat.

The retreat was of course precipitate, or it was rather, in plain terms, a flight, attended with disagreeable circumstances. The tents, with most of the artillery, fell into the hands of the garrison. It appears by the Colonel's own account that he was as apprehensive of danger from the fury of his savage allies, as he could be from the resentment of his American enemies.

It also appears from the same authority that the Messasagoes, a nation of savages to the West, plundered several of the boats belonging to the army. By the American accounts, which are in part confirmed by others, it is said that they robbed the officers of their baggage and of every other article to which they took any liking, and the army in general of their provisions. They also say that a few miles distance from the camp they first stripped of their arms and afterwards murdered with their own bayonets, all those British, German and American soldiers, who from any inability to keep up, fear or any other cause, were separated from the main body.

The state of the fact with respect to the intended relief of the fort is, that Arnold had advanced by the way of Half Moon up the Mohawk River with 2,000 men for that purpose; and that for the greater expedition he had quitted the main body and arrived by forced marches through the woods, with a detachment of 900 at the fort, on the twenty-fourth in the evening, two days after the siege had been raised. So that upon the whole the intractableness of the Indians with their watchful apprehension of danger probably saved them from a chastisement which would not have been tenderly administered.

Nothing could have been more untoward in the present situation of affairs than the unfortunate issue of this expedition. The Americans represented this and the affair at Bennington as great and glorious victories. Nothing could exceed their exultation and confidence. Ganesvoort and Willet, with General Stark and Colonel Warner, who had commanded at Bennington, were ranked among those who were considered as the saviours of their country. The northern militia began now to look high and to forget all distinctions between themselves and regular troops. As this confidence, opinion and pride increased, the apprehension of General Burgoyne's army of course declined, until it soon came to be talked of with indifference and contempt, and even its fortune to be publicly prognosticated.

The account in Andrews' *History of the War in America*, (London, 1786,) is a simple condensation from the Register. The

Dublin History borrows the identical words.

The History of an *Officer of the Army*, London, 1780, has no new authorities, and sheds no different light.

The *Impartial History of the Civil War*, London, 1780, treats the affair in the same spirit.

William Gordon, D. D., in his *History of the Rise, Progress and Establishment of the Independence of the United States of America*, (London, 1788,) claims to have had access to the papers of Washington and other American generals, and writes with the freshness of gossip. His story of Oriskany and Fort Stanwix has this character, and he states that he had some of his facts from Reverend Samuel Kirkland. Besides the references elsewhere made, he adds only a few touches of colour to this local chronicle.

15. ST. LEGER'S BOAST AND CONFIDENCE.

The following extract of a letter from Lieutenant Colonel St. Leger to Lieutenant General Burgoyne, brought through the woods by an Indian, dated before Fort Stanwix, August 11, 1777, is copied from Almon's *American Remembrancer for 1777*:

After combating the natural difficulties of the River St. Lawrence and the artificial ones the enemy threw in my way at Wood Creek, I invested Fort Stanwix the third instant. On the fifth I learnt from discovering parties on the Mohawk River that a body of one thousand militia were on their march to raise the siege. On the confirmation of this news I moved a large body of Indians, with some troops the same night, to lay in ambuscade for them on their march. They fell into it. The completest victory was obtained; above four hundred lay dead on the field, amongst the number of whom were almost all the principal movers of rebellion in that country. There are six or seven hundred men in the fort. The militia will never rally; all that I am to apprehend, therefore, that will retard my progress in joining you, is a reinforcement of what they call their regular troops, by the way of Half Moon, up the Mohawk River. A diversion, therefore, from your army by that quarter will greatly expedite my junction with either of the grand armies.

The *Remembrancer* for that year gives as a letter from Sir Guy Carleton a statement:

That Colonel St. Leger, finding Fort Stanwix too strongly fortified and the garrison too numerous to be taken by assault, and the Indians being alarmed by a false report of the approach of a large body of the rebel continental troops, he had given over the attempt of forcing a passage down the Mohawk River, and returned to Montreal, from whence he had proceeded to Ticonderoga, intending to join Lieutenant General Burgoyne by that route.

16. Bennington Counted Before Oriskany in Time.

Stedman's (British) *History of the Revolution* says:

The defeat of Colonel Baum, Breyman and St. Leger enervated the British cause in no extraordinary degree. There were many of the inhabitants not attached to either party by principle, and who had resolved to join themselves to that which should be successful. These men, after the disasters at Bennington and Stanwix, added a sudden and powerful increase of strength to the Americans.

17. Colonel Claus' Letter to Secretary Knox at London

In the eighth volume of the Documents relating to the *Colonial History of New York* is an official letter from Colonel Daniel Claus, written from Montreal, October 16, 1777, which was brought to light after all the histories of the Battle of Oriskany, which are generally familiar, were written. It is necessary to complete the record. Colonel Claus writes:

Sir: I take the liberty to give you such an account of the expedition I was appointed to this campaign, as my capacity will permit me, and which though tedious, I used all the conciseness in my power.

On my arrival at Quebec the first of June, Sir Guy Carleton being at Montreal, my letter from my Lord George Germaine was forwarded to him by Lieutenant Governor Cramahe that day, and myself arrived there a few days after. I waited upon Sir Guy, who acknowledged the receipt of the letter, but said nothing further upon it, than addressing himself to Captain Tice, who was in England with Joseph (Brant,) and there at the Levy, that I had now the command of him and those Indian officers and Indians that were destined for Brigadier St. Leger's expedition. A day or two after I waited on him again for his orders and instructions, and asked what rank I was to have on the expedition. He replied on the latter; that it could not be settled here.

Some time before our march I informed myself of Sir Guy Carleton, of the state Fort Stanwix was in; he told me that by the latest accounts from Colonel Butler, there were sixty men in a picketed place. Determined to be sure, I despatched one John Hare, an active Indian officer, with the Mohawk chief John Odiseruney, to collect a small party of Indians at Swegachy and reconnoitre Fort Stanwix, as well as possible and bring off some prisoners if they could.

On the twenty-third of June, I set out from La Chine near Montreal, The Brigadier who was getting the artillery boats ready to take in two sixes, two threes, and four Cohorns, (being our artillery for the expedition,) was to follow the day after; and proceeded for an island destined for our rendezvous in the entrance of Lake Ontario, called Buck island, in company with Sir John Johnson and his regiment. In my way thither I collected a body of a hundred and fifty Misisagey and Six Nation' Indians. All the Indians of the inhabited part of Canada whom I had under my care for fifteen years, and was best acquainted with, were destined for General Burgoyne's army. The Misisagey and Six Nations, the Brigadier intended should accompany him in an alert to Fort Stanwix, by a short cut

71

through the woods, from a place called Salmon Creek on Lake Ontario, about twenty miles from Oswego, in order to surprise the garrison and take it with small arms.

Between sixty and seventy leagues from Montreal my reconnoitring party returned and met me, with five prisoners (one lieutenant) and four scalps, having defeated a working party of sixteen rebels as they were cutting sod towards repairing and finishing the old fort, which is a regular square, and garrisoned by upwards of six hundred men, the repairs far advanced and the rebels expecting us, and were acquainted with our strength and route. I immediately forwarded the prisoners to the Brigadier who was about fifteen leagues in our rear.

On his arrival within a few leagues of Buck Island he sent for me, and, talking over the intelligence the rebel prisoners gave, he owned that if they intended to defend themselves in that fort our artillery was not sufficient to take it. However, he said, he has determined to get the truth of these fellows. I told him that having examined them separately they agreed in their story. And here the Brigadier had still an opportunity and time of sending for a better train of artillery and wait for the junction of the *Chasseurs*, which must have secured us success, as everyone will allow. However, he was still full of his *alert*, making little of the prisoners' intelligence.

On his arrival at Buck Island the eighth of July, he put me in orders as superintendent of the expedition and empowered me to act for the best of my judgment for His Majesty's service, in the management of the Indians on the expedition, as well as what regarded their equipment, presents, &c, he being an entire stranger thereto. There was then a vessel at the Island which had some Indian goods on board, which Colonel Butler had procured for the expedition, but upon examination I found that almost every one of the above articles I demanded at Montreal were deficient and a mere impossibility to procure them at Buck Island, had I not luckily provided some of those articles before I left Montreal at my own risk, and with difficulty Brigadier St. Leger found out thirty stand of arms in the artillery stores at Swegachy, and I added all my eloquence to satisfy the Indians about the rest.

The Brigadier set out from the Island upon his *alert* the nineteenth of July. I having been ordered to proceed to Oswego with Sir John Johnson's regiment and a company of *Chasseurs* lately arrived, there to convene and prepare the Indians to join the Brigadier at Fort Stanwix. On my arrival at Oswego, twenty-third July, I found Joseph Brant there, who acquainted me that his party, consisting of about three hundred Indians, would be in that day, and having been more than two months upon service, were destitute of necessaries, ammunition, and some arms.

Joseph at the same time complaining of having been very scantily supplied by Colonel Butler with ammunition when at Niagara in the spring, although he acquainted Colonel Butler of his being threatened with a visit from the rebel General Herkimer, of Tryon County, and actually was afterwards visited by him with three hundred men with him, and five hundred at some distance; when Joseph had not two hundred Indians together, but, resolutely declaring to the rebel General that he was determined to act against them for the King, he obliged them to retreat with mere menaces, not having twenty pounds of powder among his party.

The twenty-fourth of July I received an express from Brigadier St. Leger at Salmon Creek, about twenty miles from Oswego, to repair thither with what arms and vermilion I had, and that he wished I would come prepared for a march through the woods. As to arms and vermilion I had none, but prepared myself to go upon the march, and was ready to set off, when Joseph came into my tent and told me that as no person was on the spot to take care of the number of Indians with him, he apprehended in

73

case I should leave them they would become disgusted, and disperse, which might prevent the rest of the Six Nations to assemble, and be hurtful to the expedition, and begged I would first represent these circumstances to the Brigadier by letter.

Brigadier St. Leger mentioned indeed, my going was chiefly intended to quiet the Indians with him, who were very drunk and riotous, and Captain Tice, who was the messenger, informed me that the Brigadier ordered the Indians a quart of rum apiece, which made them all beastly drunk, and in which case it is not in the power of man to quiet them. Accordingly I mentioned to the Brigadier by letter the consequences that might affect His Majesty's Indian interest in case I was to leave so large a number of Indians that were come already and still expected. Upon which representation and finding the Indians disapproved of the plan, and were unwilling to proceed, the Brigadier came away from Salmon Creek and arrived the next day at Oswego with the companies of the eighth and thirty-fourth regiments and about two hundred and fifty Indians.

Having equipped Joseph's party with what necessaries and ammunition I had, I appointed the rest of the Six Nations to assemble at the Three Rivers,. a convenient place of rendezvous, and in the way to Fort Stanwix, and desired Colonel Butler to follow me with the Indians he brought with him from Niagara, and equip them all at the Three Rivers.

The twenty-sixth of July left Oswego, and second of August arrived with the Brigadier and the greatest part of the troops before Fort Stanwix, which was invested the same evening. The enemy having stopped up a narrow river, called Wood Creek, by cutting of trees across it for about twenty miles, along which our artillery, provisions and baggage were to pass, which passage to cut open required a number of men, as well as cutting a road through the woods for twenty-five miles, to bring up the artillery, stores, &c, that were immediately wanted, which weakened our small army greatly.

The third, fourth and fifth the Indians surrounded the fort and fired from behind logs and rising grounds, at the garrison, wherever they had an object, which prevented them from working at the fortifications in the day. The fifth, in the afternoon, accounts were brought by Indians, sent by Joseph's sister from Canajoharie, that a body of rebels were on their march and would be within ten or twelve miles of our camp at night. A detachment of about four hundred Indians was ordered to reconnoitre the enemy. Sir John Johnson asked leave to join his company of light infantry and head the whole, which was granted. Colonel Butler and other Indian officers were ordered with the Indians.

The rebels having an imperfect account of the number of Indians that joined us, (being upward of eight hundred,) not thinking them by one-fourth as many, and being sure as to our strength and artillery, (which we learned by prisoners,) that they knew it from their emissaries before we left Canada, They therefore, on the sixth, marched on, to the number of upwards of eight hundred, with security and carelessness.

When within six miles of the Fort they were waylaid by our party, surprised, briskly attacked, and after a little resistance, repulsed and defeated; leaving upwards of five hundred killed on the spot, among which were their principal officers and ringleaders; their general was shot through the knee, and a few days afterward died of an amputation.

We lost Captains Hare and Wilson of the Indians, Lieutenant McDonald of Sir John's regiment, two or three privates and thirty-two Indians, among which were several Seneka chiefs killed. Captain Watts, Lieutenant Singleton of Sir John's regiment, and thirty-three Indians wounded.

During the action when the garrison found the Indians' camp (who went out against their reinforcement) empty, they boldly sallied out with three hundred men, and two field pieces, and took away the Indians' packs, with their cloths, *wampum* and silver work, "they having gone in their shirts, as naked to action;" and when they found a party advancing from our camp, they returned with their spoil, taking with them Lieutenant Singleton and a private of Sir John's regiment, who lay wounded in the Indian camp.

The disappointment was rather greater to the Indians than their loss, for they had nothing to cover themselves at night, or against the weather, and nothing in our camp to supply them till I got to Oswego.

After this defeat and having got part of our artillery up, some cohorn shells were thrown into the fort, and a few shots fired. A flag then was sent with an account of the disaster of their intended relief, and the garrison was summoned to surrender prisoners of war, to be marched down the country, leaving baggage, &c, behind, to satisfy the Indians for their losses.

The rebels knowing their strength in garrison, as well as fortification, and the insufficiency of our field pieces to hurt them, and apprehensive of being massacred by the Indians for the losses they sustained in the action; they rejected the summons and said they were determined to hold out to the extremity.

The siege then was carried on with as much vigour as possible for nineteen days, but to no purpose. Sir John Johnson proposed to follow the blow given to the reinforcement, (who were chiefly Mohawk River people,) to march down the country with about two hundred men, and I intended joining him with a sufficient body of Indians; but the Brigadier said he could not spare the men, and disapproved of it. The inhabitants in general were ready (as we afterwards learned) to submit and come in. A flag then was sent to invite the inhabitants to submit and be forgiven, and assurance given to prevent the Indians from being outrageous; but the commanding officer of the German Flats hearing of it, seized the flag, consisting of Ensign Butler of the Eighth Regiment, ten soldiers and three Indians, and took them up as spies.

A few days after General Arnold, coming with some cannon and a reinforcement, made the inhabitants return to their obedience. The Indians, finding that our besieging the fort was of no effect, our troops but few, a reinforcement, as was reported, of fifteen hundred or two thousand men, with field pieces by the way, began to be dispirited and fell off by degrees. The chiefs advised the Brigadier to retreat to Oswego and get better artillery from Niagara, and more men, and so return and renew the siege; to which the Brigadier agreed, and accordingly retreated on the twenty-second of August.

On our arrival at Oswego the twenty-sixth and examining into the state of the troops' necessaries, the men were without shoes and other things which only could be got at Montreal, the Brigadier at the same time having received a letter from General Burgoyne to join him, either by a march through the woods back of Tryon County, (which was impracticable,) or the way he came. He adopted the latter on account of procuring necessaries for the men. The Indians were as much as possible reconciled to this resolution, with a promise that they should be convened as soon as Colonel Butler could return from Montreal with some necessaries for them. There being Indian traders at Oswego, I saw myself under a necessity to clothe those Indians that lost their packs by the rebels at Fort Stanwix, which made them return home contented.

Thus has an expedition miscarried merely for want of timely and good intelligence. For it is impossible to believe that had the Brigadier St. Leger known the real state of the fort and garrison of Fort Stanwix, he could possibly have proceeded from Montreal without a sufficient train of artillery and his full complement of troops. And yet by what I find, very large sums have been expended on account of government at Niagara upon the Indians these two years past, and they at the same time kept inactive; whereas, had these presents been properly applied, the Six Nations might not only prevent Fort Stanwix from being re-established, but even let not a rebel come near it or keep it up; it being almost in the heart of their country, and they with reluctance saw the Crown erect a fort there last war.

All the good done by the expedition was, that the ring-leaders and principal men of the rebels of Tryon County were put out of the way; but had we succeeded it must be of vast good effect to the Northern operations, and its miscarrying, I apprehend, to my deep concern, to be the reverse.

18. ROSTER OF ORISKANY.

For several weeks in June and July, 1877, the *Utica Herald* appealed to descendants of those engaged in the battle, and to all others, for names to make up a Roster of Oriskany, to preserve the names of all persons who took part in that important action. As the sum of its efforts, from all sources, that journal gathered the following list:

ROSTER OF ORISKANY.

* Brigadier General NICHOLAS HERKIMER, Danube; Captain GEORGE HERKI-MER, Danube; * FREDERICK AYER, (Oyer) Schuyler; ‡ Major BLAUVELT, Mohawk ; † Captain GEORGE HENRY BELL, Fall Hill; * JOSEPH BELL, Fall Hill; NICHOLAS BELL, Fall Hill; † Captain JOHN BREADBEG, Palatine; ADAM BELLINGER; Colonel JOHN BELLINGER, Utica; Colonel PETER BELLINGER, German Flats; ‡ Lieutenant Colonel FREDERICK BELLINGER, German Flats; * SAMUEL BILLINGTON, Palatine, Committee of Safety ; —— BILLINGTON, Palatine; * Major JOHN BLEVIN; † Captain JACOB BOWMAN, Canajoharie; JOHN BOYER; Lieutenant Colonel SAMUEL CAMPBELL, Cherry Valley ; * Lieutenant ROBERT CAMPBELL, Cherry Valley; Major SAMUEL CLYDE, Cherry Valley; JACOB CASTLER; JOHN CASTLER; ADAM CASSLER; JACOB CLEMENS, Schuyler; Captain A. COPEMAN, Minden; RICHARD COPPERNOLL; Colonel EBENEZER COX, Canajoharie; WILLIAM COX ; * ROBERT CROUSE, Canajoharie ; * BENJAMIN DAVIS; * Captain JOHN DAVIS, Mohawk; MARTINUS DAVIS, Mohawk; NICHOLAS DE-

GRAFF, Amsterdam ; Captain MARX DeMUTH, Deerfield ; *Captain ANDREW DILLENBACK, Palatine ; JOHN DOXTADER, German Flats ; Captain HENRY DIEFENDORF, Canajoharie ; HON (JOHN) PETER DUNCKEL, Freysbush ; HON GARRET DUNCKEL, Freysbush ; HON NICHOLAS DUNCKEL, Freysbush ; FRANCIS DUNCKEL, Freysbush ; *JOHN DYGERT, Committee of Safety ; Captain WILLIAM DYGERT, German Flats ; * Major JOHN EISENLORD, Stone Arabia ; PETER EHLE, Palatine ; JACOB EMPIE, Palatine ; HENRY FAILING, Canajoharie ; JELLES FONDA ; Captain ADAM FONDA ; VALENTINE FRALICK, Palatine ; ‡ Major JOHN FREY, Palatine ; *Captain CHRISTOPHER P. FOX, Palatine ; Captain CHRISTOPHER W. FOX, Palatine ; CHARLES FOX, Palatine ; PETER FOX, Palatine ; CHRISTOPHER FOX, Palatine ; GEORGE GEORTNER, Canajoharie ; Captain LAWRENCE GROS, Minden ; *NICHOLAS GRAY, Palatine ; Lieutenant SAMUEL GRAY, Herkimer ; Captain —— GRAVES ; Captain JACOB GARDINIER, Mohawk ; Lieutenant SAMUEL GARDINIER, Mohawk ; Lieutenant PETRUS GROOT, Amsterdam ; HENRY HARTER, German Flats ; JOHN ADAM HARTMAN, Herkimer ; JOHN ADAM HELMER, German Flats ; *Captain FREDERICK HELMER, German Flats ; JOHN HEYCK, Palatine ; NICHOLAS HILL ; Lieutenant YOST HOUSE, Minden ; CHRISTIAN HUFFNAIL, Minden ; *Lieutenant Colonel ABEL HUNT, Canajoharie ; ANDREW KELLER, Palatine ; JACOB KELLER, Palatine ; SOLOMON KELLER, Palatine ; *Major DENNIS KLAPSATTLE, German Flats ; JACOB KLAPSATTLE, German Flats ; PETER KILTS, Palatine ; Colonel JACOB G. KLOCK, Palatine ; GEORGE LIGHTHALL, Minden ; GEORGE LINTNER, Minden ; HENRY LONUS, Minden ; SOLOMON LONGSHORE, Canajoharie ; *JACOB MARKELL, Springfield ; *WILLIAM MERCKLEY, Palatine ; JOHN P. MILLER, Minden ; JACOB MOYER, (now MYERS, German Flats ; Lieutenant DAVID McMASTER, Florida ; ADAM MILLER, Minden ; HENRY MILLER, Minden ; DAVID MURRAY, Fonda ; CHRISTIAN NELLES ; JOHN D. NELLIS, Palatine ; PETER NESTLE, Palatine ; *Honorable ISAAC PARIS, Palatine, and his son who was also killed ; JOHN NIARRI PETRI, Fort Herkimer ; *Lieutenant DEDERIAH MARX PETRIE, Herkimer ; Doctor WILLIAM PETRY, Fort Herkimer, Committee of Safety ; ‡JOSEPH PETRY, Dayton ; *Captain SAMUEL PETTINGILL, Mohawk ; ‡ ADAM PRICE, Minden ; NICHOLAS PICKARD, Minden ; RICHARD PUTNAM, Mohawk ; ABRAHAM D. QUACKENBOSS ; ‡JACOB RACHIOUR, Minden ; GEORGE RAYNOR, Minden ; Captain NICHOLAS RECTOR, Garoga ; JOHN ROOF ; JOHN ROTHER ; MARK RASPACH, Kingsland ; HENRY SANDERS, Minden ; SAMSON SAMMONS, Fonda, Committee of Safety ; JACOB SAMMONS, Fonda ; *WILLIAM SCHAVER ; Ensign JOHN YOST SCHOLL, Palatine ; *Colonel SAFFRENESS SEEBER, Canajoharie ; ‡Captain JACOB SEEBER, Canajoharie ; ‡Lieutenant WILLIAM SEEBER, Canajoharie ; ‡HENRY SEEBER, Canajoharie ; *JAMES SEEBER, Canajoharie ; Lieutenant JOHN SEEBER, Minden ; *AUDOLPH SEEBER, Minden ; PETER SITZ, Palatine ; RUDOLPH SIEBERT ; HENRY SPENCER, Indian Interpreter ; CHRISTIAN SCHELL, Little Falls ; GEORGE SMITH, Palatine ; Colonel HENRY STARING, Schuyler ; Captain RUDOLPH SHOEMAKER, Canajoharie ; *JOSEPH SNELL, Snellbush, now Manheim ; *JACOB SNELL, Snellbush ; PETER SNELL, Snellbush ; GEORGE SNELL, Snellbush ; *JOHN SNELL, Stone Arabia ; * JOHN SNELL, Jr., Stone Arabia ; * FREDERICK SNELL, Snellbush ; Lieutenant JEREMIAH SWARTS, Mohawk ; JOHN G. SILLENBECK ; JOHN SHULTS, Palatine ; GEORGE SHULTS, Stone Arabia ; PEPER SUMMER ; ADAM THUMB, Palatine ; JACOB TIMMERMAN, St. Johnsville ; Lieutenant HENRY TIMMERMAN, St. Johnsville ; HENRY THOMPSON, Fultonville ; Lieutenant MARTIN C. VAN ALSTYNE, Canajoharie; *JOHN VAN ANTWERP; GEORGE VAN DEUSEN, Canajoharie; HENRY VEDDER; †CONRAD VOLS, (now FOLTZ,) German Flats; Lieutenant JACOB VOLS, German Flats; *Major HARMANUS VAN SLYCK, Palatine; *Major NICHOLAS VAN SLYCK; Colonel FREDERICK VISSCHER, Mohawk; Captain JOHN VISSCHER, Mohawk; ‡Lieutenant Colonel HENRY WALRADT, German Flats; GARRETT WALRATH, German Flats; GEORGE WALTER, Palatine; Lieutenant Colonel PETER WAGGONER, Palatine; Lieutenant PETER WAGGONER, Jr., Palatine; GEORGE WAGGONER, Palatine; JOHN WAGGONER, Palatine; JACOB WAGNER, Canajoharie; JOHN WAGNER, Canajoharie; PETER WESTERMAN, Canajoharie; *JOHN WOLLOVER, Fort Herkimer; ABRAHAM WOLLOVER, Fort Herkimer; †PETER WOLLOVER, Fort Herkimer; *RICHARD WOLLOVER, Fort Herkimer; JACOB WEVER, German Flats; PETER JAMS WEAVER, German Flats; MICHAEL WIDRICK, Schuyler; *LAWRENCE WRENKLE, Fort Herkimer; †Doctor MOSES YOUNGLOVE, Surgeon; Captain ROBERT YATES; †NICHOLAS YERDON, Minden.

* Killed.   † Wounded.   ‡ Taken prisoner.

The regiments as stated in the text, were raised by districts. Tryon County had four. The Mohawk district lay lowest down the river. Next west, and to the south of the river, was the Canajoharie district, reaching to Little Falls and to Cherry Valley. Palatine district lay north of the river, and extended west from the Mohawk district to Little Falls. The district of German Flats and Kingsland included all the territory west of Little Falls on both sides of the river.

Colonel Cox's regiment had been ordered to Ticonderoga in the preceding winter, as the manuscript narrative of Frederick Sammons, states. It is now in the possession of Colonel Simeon Sammons, of Fonda, who has kindly permitted the writer to peruse it.

Fort Schuyler, Oriskany and Bennington, 1777

(Extract from *Battles of the American Revolution* by Henry Beebee Carrington)

The month of August, 1777, developed and concluded the expedition of Colonel St. Leger to the valley of the Mohawk River, and with equal exactness terminated the operations of Burgoyne on the eastern bank of the Hudson.

St. Leger ascended the River St. Lawrence and Lake Ontario, ascended the Oswego and Oneida Rivers to Oneida Lake, crossed that lake, and found himself on Fish Creek, within a few miles of Fort Stanwix, (Schuyler) near the present city of Rome, on the Mohawk River. It is to be noticed that with the exception of the short portage between Fish Creek and the Mohawk, there was water communication for light boats and *bateaux* from Oswego to Albany. The intervening streams were all subject to the fluctuations of wet and dry seasons, but the burden of military transportation was greatly lightened by the character of the route adopted for the invasion of New York from the west.

The character of the settlers in that region, particularly in Tryon County, had fostered loyal sentiments, and the diversities of interest among the various Indian tribes involved a constant uncertainty as to the integrity of their conduct, no matter what might be the terms of a contract into which they could be enticed by high sounding promises and presents.

Notwithstanding the protracted negotiations and repeated interviews of General Schuyler with the Six Nations, the Oneidas alone remained neutral in the campaign under notice.

Fort Schuyler, at the bend of the Mohawk River from a southerly to an easterly course, was commanded by Colonel Peter Gansevoort, as early as April, 1777. He found that it was actually untenable against any enemy whatever. Although in doubt whether to provide for resistance to artillery, he went to work with such industry, that when the test was made, it proved fully adequate to withstand the fire of the light ordnance which accompanied the column of St. Leger in August of that year.

On the twenty-ninth of May, Colonel Marinus Willett was ordered to report with his regiment for duty at the same post, and to aid in putting the fort in a thoroughly defensive condition. He reached Fort Schuyler in July. On the second of August five *bateaux* arrived with sufficient stores to increase the rations and small-arm ammunition to a supply for six weeks. The garrison then numbered seven hundred and fifty men. Lieut.-Col. Mellon, of Colonel Wesson's Massachusetts regiment, with two hundred men, accompanied the *bateaux* as their escort, and joined the garrison. On the same day, and within an hour after the landing of this timely invoice of supplies, Lieutenant Bird of the British Eighth regiment approached the fort, and established a position for St. Leger's advanced guard; and on the third of August his army began the investment.

The advance of St. Leger was conspicuous for its excellent adjustments. This was largely due to the presence of those who had skill in frontier Indian warfare. The entire force was so disposed by single files and the wise distribution of the Indian auxiliaries, as to make a surprise impossible, and afford the best possible opportunity for their peculiar style of skirmishing warfare, in case of an attack. Stone's *Life of Brant* very clearly represents this movement, and Lossing reproduces it with full details of the antecedent Indian operations in central New York.

Colonel Daniel Claus, son-in-law of Sir William Johnson; Colonel John Butler, afterward conspicuous at the massacre of Wyoming; Joseph Brant, a full-blooded Mohawk, son of a Wolf tribe chief; and Sir John Johnson, a son of Sir William Johnson,

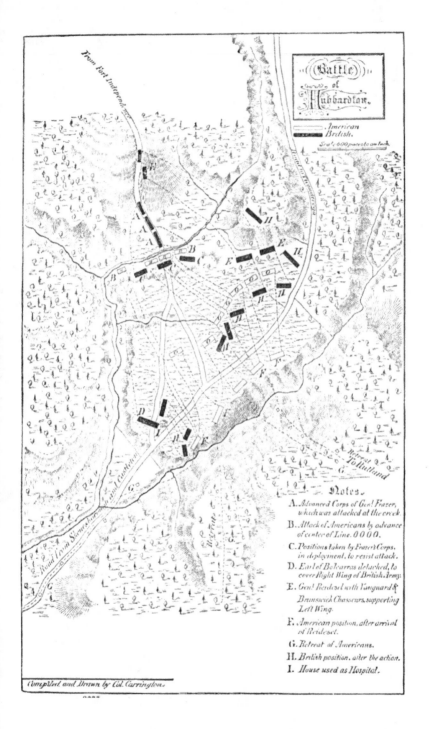

From Fort Independence

((Battle)) of Hubbardton.

American
British.
Scale 600 paces to an Inch

Road from Shoreham and Castleton

Retreat to Rutland

Brigade

Notes.

A. Advanced Corps of Gen! Frazer, which was attacked at the creek.

B. Attack of Americans by advance of center of Line. 0 0 0 0

C. Positions taken by Frazer's Corps, in deployment, to resist attack.

D. Earl of Balcarras detached, to cover Right Wing of British Army.

E. Gen! Redesel with Vanguard & Brunswick Chasseurs, supporting Left Wing.

F. American position, after arrival of Redesel.

G. Retreat of Americans.

H. British position, after the action.

I. House used as Hospital.

Compiled and Drawn by Col. Carrington.

who succeeded to the title in 1774, were associated with St. Leger in command of this composite army of regulars, Hessian-*chasseurs*, Royal-greens, Canadians, axe-men, and non-combatants, who, as well as the Indians, proved an ultimate incumbrance and curse to the expedition. The investment was immediate. A proclamation of St. Leger, was followed by an appeal from General Nicholas Herkimer to the militia of Tryon County, and on the sixth he passed three scouts into the fort, with notice that he was at Oriskany, near the present village of Whitesborough, with eight hundred men advancing to its relief. He also requested that three guns might be fired to give notice of the safe arrival of his couriers. Colonel Willett, as had been suggested by General Herkimer, promptly sallied forth with two hundred and fifty men, portions of Gansevoort's, and of Wesson's regiments, and one iron three pounder, to make a diversion in favour of the advancing militia.

St. Leger had been advised of this movement of the militia, and was so engaged in preparation to attack it in the woods, and had so large a fatigue detail at work upon the intrenchments, as to have entirely ignored the possibility of offensive action on the part of the garrison. The sortie was therefore successful in the capture of much camp plunder, such as blankets, arms, flags, and clothing, a few prisoners, St. Leger's desk and papers, and the destruction of two sections of the intrenchments; but failed to unite with General Herkimer. That officer, overborne in his judgment by the impetuosity of younger officers, who mistook his caution in approaching the Indian camp for cowardice, allowed his march to be crowded too rapidly, and while crossing a ravine near Oriskany Creek, he fell into an ambuscade which involved great slaughter.

General Herkimer himself was severely wounded, and the total American casualties were not less than one hundred and sixty killed, besides more than two hundred wounded, and some prisoners. The Indian loss in killed and wounded was nearly eighty, including several valuable warriors, and the field was abandoned by the assailants. Colonel St. Leger made no official report of his loss, except that of his Indian allies. The fight continued for several hours, only suspended for a short time by a thunder storm, and stands on record as one of the most fiercely contested conflicts of the war.

On the afternoon of the seventh, St. Leger demanded the surrender of the post, under threat of giving over its garrison to the vengeance of the Indians. A bold defiance was the sole response. He also wrote to Burgoyne on the eleventh, that "he was secure of the fort and would soon join him at Albany."

On the tenth Colonel Willett, afterwards active at Monmouth and in subsequent Indian wars, and Lieutenant Stockwell, smuggled themselves through the lines, and reached Fort Dayton (now Herkimer) safely, to arouse the militia to fresh efforts in behalf of the post. General Schuyler had already ordered General Learned's Massachusetts brigade on this duty, designating Fort Dayton as the rendezvous for the relief of Fort Schuyer. Colonel Willett went directly to Albany, and returned in company with Arnold and the first New York regiment; but while the troops were yet forty miles distant from Fort Dayton, St. Leger, alarmed by reports of Arnold's march and rumours of a disaster to Burgoyne's army, precipitately abandoned his intrenchments and fled to Oswego, leaving a portion of his artillery, baggage and camp equipage on the field. In his official report, dated at Oswego, August twenty-seventh, St. Leger explained his retreat by charges of treachery and exaggerated reports of Arnold's force, closing with the suggestive statement that his own men "are in a most deplorable situation from the plunder of the savages."

Thus ended the British advance upon Albany, by the Mohawk valley. The moral effect of its failure was as encouraging to the American army, as the tidings of its advent, coupled with the successes of Burgoyne, had been depressing; and the animation of the army was fully shared by the people.

General Washington wrote as follows to General Schuyler, on the twenty-first of August, when advised of the Battle of Oriskany and of his detail of General Arnold to the relief of Fort Schuyler:

I am pleased with the account you transmit of the situation of matters upon the Mohawk river. If the militia keep up their spirits after the late severe skirmish, I am confident they will, with the assistance of the reinforcements under General Arnold, be enabled to raise the siege of Fort Schuyler, which will be a most important matter just at this time.

At the time when St. Leger established his camp before Fort Schuyler, General Burgoyne began to realize the difficulties which attended the supply of his army. He had received altogether, are inforcement of nearly a thousand Indians, but the murder of Miss Jane McCrea and repeated violations of the usages of civilized war fare, as well as the additional mouths to feed, increased the discomfort and embarrassment of his position. The reports of German officers to their sovereigns, abound in descriptions of the horrors of this warfare. One wrote, that "to prevent desertions it was announced in orders that the savages would scalp runaways."

Schlöozer states, that "on the third of August, they, the Indians, brought in twenty scalps and as many captives." It is clear that there was no responsibility on the part of Burgoyne for the murder of Miss McCrea, or other personal violence, and a careful sifting of all accessible reports as clearly shows that most of the outrages reported at the time were exaggerations of a style of warfare which was under as good control as possible under any commander. The Indians could not be civilized instantly, nor be readily made to acquiesce in the limit of rations which was assigned to regular troops, and all their demands were of the most imperative kind.

Burgoyne thus states his own views upon this subject, "I had been taught to look upon the remote tribes which joined me at Skenesborough, as more warlike:—but, with equal depravity in general principles, their only pre-eminence consisted in ferocity." He also experienced difficulty in managing *Indian agents*, and thus expresses a sentiment which will be appreciated by all officers who have engaged in frontier Indian service, where interpreters and intermediate civil agents are employed.

The interpreters, from the first, regarded with a jealous eye a system which took out of their hands the distribution of Indian necessaries and presents; but when they found the plunder of the country, as well as that of the government, was *controlled*, the profligacy of many was employed to promote dissension, revolt and desertion. Although I differed totally with St. Luc, 'then in general charge of the Indian auxiliaries,' in opinion upon the efficiency of these allies, I invariably took his advice in the management of them, even to an indulgence of their most capricious fancies, when they did not involve the dishonour of the King's cause and the disgrace of humanity.

He certainly knew that the Indians pined after a renewal of their accustomed horrors and that they were become as impatient of *his* control as of any other: though the pride and interest of authority and the affection he bore his old associates induced him to cover the real causes, under various pretenses of discontent with which I was daily tormented.

At a council held August fourth, it appeared that the tribes with which St. Luc was immediately connected and for which he interpreted, were determined to go home. Burgoyne thus writes to Lord Germaine:

I was convinced that a cordial reconciliation with the Indians was only to be effected by a renunciation of all my former prohibitions and indulgence in blood and rapine.

Many of the Indians did in fact leave the next day, and many others before the expedition to Bennington was planned, so that the loss of valuable scouts and skirmishers was greatly felt during operations in the forests on the line of that march. An additional statement of General Burgoyne is properly recorded to his permanent credit.

The Indian principle of war is at once odious and unavailing, and if encouraged, I will venture to pronounce, its consequences will be severely repented by the present age, and universally abhorred by posterity.

This statement was made before the House of Commons, but that it was not an after-thought, is clearly seen from the statement made by Burgoyne to St. Luc, in the presence of the Earl of Harrington: "I would rather lose every Indian, than connive at their enormities."

St. Luc was angry because Burgoyne insisted that a British officer should accompany all Indian forays, and take account of their proceedings and their plunder; and several parties were brought into his camp as prisoners, who affirmed that they had been treated with proper clemency. It was not until this rule was enforced that St. Luc stirred up the Indians to desertion and outrage. He is not a competent witness in the case.

The following entry appears upon Burgoyne's record:

August fifth. Victualling of the army *out* this day, and from difficulties of the roads and transports, no provisions came in this night. Sixth August. At ten o'clock this morning, not quite enough provisions for the consumption of two days.

In this emergency advantage was taken of the statement of Philip Skene, whose co-operation brought mischief only to the expedition, and of others supported by scouts sent out by General Riedesel, that a large depot of commissary supplies had been accumulated at Bennington for the American army, and an expedition was organized for the threefold purpose of securing these supplies, procuring thirteen hundred horses for mounting Riedesel's dragoons and Peter's corps, and two hundred for general army use, and of making a demonstration in the Connecticut River valley.

On the ninth, carefully written instructions were prepared for Lieutenant-colonel Baume, who was intrusted with the command of the expedition, and these were so judiciously framed as to anticipate all possible contingencies of the march. They took into view the fact that Colonel Warner was still at Manchester, and the possibility that Arnold s main army, at that time suggested for a proposed movement to Burgoyne's rear, might attempt to intercept his return march.

In view of the exceptions taken to the assignment of German troops to this expedition, it is in evidence that even General Fraser, who considered the Germans as *slow*, declined to suggest to General Burgoyne the substitution of other troops, although asked to do so by Adjutant-general Kingston, "if he thought other troops should be detailed," remarking "the Germans are not a very active people, but it may do." This matter was especially submitted to General Fraser, "because the scouts and guides were attached to his, the advanced corps, and it was thought that he might know more of the nature of the country." There was no declared difference of opinion among the general officers as to the value and wisdom of the expedition itself. It was to comprehend Arlington, lying between Manchester and Bennington, and as wide a scope of country as would afford opportunity to overawe the people and secure supplies, and was allowed a margin of two weeks' time, with adequate instructions in case the main army should advance towards Albany before its return.

Burgoyne thus states the case:

It was soon found that in the situation of the transport-service at that time, the army could barely be victualed from day to day, and that there was no prospect of establishing a magazine in due time for pursuing present advantages. The idea of the expedition to Bennington originated upon this difficulty, combined with the intelligence reported by General Riedesel, and with all I had otherwise received. I knew that Bennington was the great deposit of corn, flour, and store cattle, that it was only guarded by militia, and every day's account tended to confirm the persuasion of the loyalty of one description of inhabitants and the panic of the other. Those who knew the country best were the most sanguine in this persuasion. The German troops employed were of the best I had of that nation. The number of British was small, but it was the select light corps of the army, composed of chosen men from all the regiments, and commanded by Captain Fraser, one of the most distinguished officers in his line of service that I ever met with.

An additional statement is necessary at this stage of the narrative, to show exactly the status of the British army, in the matter of Logistics.

Fort Edward was sixteen miles from Fort George. Only one haul could be made each day. Six miles below Fort Edward were rapids which required a transfer of all stores to boats below; and the un loaded boats had to be hauled back against a strong current. The horses from Canada came by land from St. John's to Ticonderoga, through a country then hardly less than a desert, and the whole number of carts and horses at that time received, was barely enough to keep the army in supplies.

As early as May thirtieth, while at Montreal, an order was issued that blanket-coats, leggings, and all clothing but summer wear should be left behind, and before leaving Skenesborough the officers were ordered to send all their personal baggage to Ticonderoga, except a soldier s common tent and a cloak-bag.

The roads, bridges, quagmires, and rocks were constant causes of delay in hauling stores. Heavy rains set in. Ten and twelve oxen were often required to haul a single bateaux, and only fifty head had been procured for the entire army use. There was no remedy but patience, no honourable retreat, no alternative but to make the most of the present, and press toward Albany and the anticipated union with General Howe and St. Leger.

On the fourteenth of August, a bridge of rafts was thrown across the river at Saratoga, where the vanguard of the British army had been established, to be in position for an advance upon Albany as soon as the supplies should be realized from the expedition then on the move. Lieutenant-colonel Breyman's corps was posted at Batten-kill, to be in readiness to render support to that of Lieutenant-colonel Baume if it became necessary.

Lieutenant-colonel Baume himself marched, on the eleventh, with two hundred dismounted dragoons of the regiment of Riedesel, Captain Eraser's marksmen, Peter's Provincials, the Canadian volunteers, and something over one hundred Indians, making, as stated by Burgoyne, a total strength of about five hundred men.

He halted at Batten-kill to await orders, where General Burgoyne inspected the command; and he expressed himself satisfied with the force placed at his disposal. In a note from his camp, he adds this postscript:

> The *reinforcement of fifty chasseurs* which your Excellency was pleased to order, joined me last night at eleven o clock.

After marching sixteen miles, he reached Cambridge at four o'clock in the afternoon of the thirteenth, and reported a skirmish with forty or fifty rebels who were guarding cattle; and stated that the enemy were reported to be eighteen hundred strong at Bennington. He also stated that "the savages would destroy or drive away all horses for which he did not pay the money," and asked authority to purchase the horses thus taken by the savages, "otherwise they will ruin all they meet with, and neither officers nor interpreters can control them." This express started from Cambridge at four o'clock of the morning of the fourteenth.

The letter closed:

> Your Excellency may depend on hearing how I proceed at Bennington, and of my success there. I will be particularly careful on my approach to that place to be fully informed of their strength and position, and take the precautions necessary to fulfil both the orders and instructions of your Excellency.

Burgoyne replied, August fourteenth at seven at night, instructing fully as to the items of the dispatch received, adding, "should you find the enemy too strongly posted at Bennington,

I wish you to take a post where you can maintain yourself till you receive an answer from me, and I will either support you in force, or withdraw you."

On the fourteenth at nine o'clock, he reported from Sancoick (Van Schaick's Mills) of a skirmish, the capture of flour, salt, etc., that "five prisoners agree that from fifteen to eighteen hundred men are at Bennington, but are supposed to leave on our approach," adding, "I will proceed so far today as to fall on the enemy tomorrow early, and make such disposition as I think necessary from the intelligence I receive. People are flocking in hourly, but want to be armed; the savages cannot be controlled. They ruin and take everything they please."

> *Postscript.* Beg your Excellency to pardon the hurry of this letter, as it is wrote on the head of a barrel.

This was the last dispatch from Baume, and no reinforcements were called for, neither was there intimation that they would be required. Careful examination fails to find the data upon which many historians make the statement. The record of this message made at headquarters is as follows:

> 15th August, express arrived from Sancoick at five o'clock in the morning. *Corps de reserve* ordered to march.

General Burgoyne promptly and wisely started Breyman's force of five hundred men to the support of Baume as soon as advised that the "secret expedition had been discovered by the enemy, and that the American force was probably greater than he had before anticipated."

Colonel Breyman received his orders at eight o'clock on the morning of the fifteenth, and marched at nine, with one battalion of *chasseurs*, one of grenadiers, one rifle company and two pieces of cannon.

> Each soldier carried forty rounds of ammunition in his pouch, and on account of the scarcity of transportation, two boxes of ammunition were placed upon the artillery carts.

This command met with constant disaster. A heavy rain continued during the day, so that the troops made but a half English mile an hour: the guns had to be hauled up hills, alternately; one artillery cart was overturned; a timbrel was broken up and its ammunition wasted; the guide lost his way, and at night the detachment was still seven miles from Cambridge. Lieutenant Hanneman was sent forward to inform Lieutenant-colonel Baume of the approach of reinforcements.

Breyman reached Van Schaick's mill at half past four o'clock in the afternoon, where he met Colonel Skene, who notified him that Baume was two miles in advance. He pushed on to his support with no intimation that any engagement had taken place.

> At the bridge, a force of men was met, some in jackets and some in shirts, whom Skene declared to be royalists, but they proved to be rebels, attempting to gain high ground to his left.

> A vigorous attack was made, with varying success and lasting until nearly eight o'clock. The ammunition was expended, the horses had been killed, Lieutenant Spangenburg and many others were wounded, and the American forces were constantly adding to their numbers. The guns were abandoned. The troops reached Cambridge at twelve o'clock and regained camp on the morning of the seventeenth.

Such is the melancholy summary of Breyman's report, closing, "could I have saved my cannon I would with pleasure have sacrificed my life to have effected it."

General Stark had returned to New Hampshire some time after the battle of Trenton, on a recruiting expedition, and resigned his commission upon hearing that Congress had promoted junior officers over his head. The appeal of his native State was not to be resisted when the invasion of Burgoyne took place; and he accepted a command, upon condition that he should not be compelled to join the main army.

General Lincoln visited Manchester, where recruits were assembling, with an order from General Schuyler for Stark to report for duty; but could not induce him to swerve from his purpose. He was at Bennington on the night of the thirtieth, when advised that a body of Indians had reached Cambridge. Colonel Gregg was at once sent with two hundred men to oppose their advance. During the night an express messenger brought word that a large force of British troops was on the march, of which the Indians constituted only the van guard. He immediately sent to Colonel Warner, then at Manchester, an appeal for aid, aroused the militia, and made preparations to meet the enemy.

On the fourteenth Lieutenant-colonel Baume advanced to within four miles of Bennington. The Americans, unprepared for battle, retired before his advance, and encamped on the Bennington road, (see map). General Burgoyne in his report states that:

> Lieutenant-colonel Baume sacrificed his command by violation of orders, in continuing his advance when met by superior numbers, and by too widely scattering his force.

The embarrassment of Baume was two-fold. His force was not homogeneous; and his adversary was too strong. He followed orders quite literally in holding his dragoons together and using the Provincials and other irregular troops as pickets, but the latter were a mile from his own position and there was no possibility of concert of action in defence.

He occupied a commanding hill quite thickly wooded at a bend of the Walloomscoick, and at once intrenched his position. On the fifteenth, the rain which retarded the march of Breyman suspended active operations, except skirmishing; but Colonel Warner made the march from Manchester, and Colonel Symonds arrived at Bennington with a detachment of Berkshire militia, so that on the morning of the sixteenth the force of General Stark amounted to nearly or quite two thousand men.

Colonel Warner's regiment halted at Bennington to rest from their march and dry their arms and equipments, while Stark so distributed the regiments of his own brigade and the militia, as to be ready in the morning for the assault, which, after conference with his officers, he had already arranged. Riedesel's dragoons with a part of the rangers occupied the summit already referred to; while one company advanced down the slope, to cover the *chasseurs*, who were near the foot of the hill where a small creek enters the Walloomscoick. One company of grenadiers, with a portion of the rangers, occupied a position behind the bridge, on the road to Bennington, and the Canadians with a detachment of Royalist Americans, took possession of houses south of the bridge, and a slight elevation lower down, near the ford, where a trench was hastily dug for partial protection.

A second detachment of grenadiers and royalists occupied the extreme British right, in open ground to the northwest, at the foot of the hill near the Saratoga road. A portion of the Indian scouts took position on the opposite side of the road, on their first arrival, but they fled on the fourteenth, as soon as the Americans were found to be in force. The remainder who encamped in the woods to the rear of Baume, broke away between the advancing columns of Nichols and Herrick as soon as the battle began on the sixteenth.

General Stark reserved for himself the direct attack up the steepest part of the hill, and held his men in hand until the other troops took their assigned positions. Nichols struck the British left. Herrick took their extreme right, in the rear. Stickney cut off the detachments at the bridge from union with Baume ;and Hubbard with equal spirit attacked the positions held in advance of the bridge. These attacks were made with great promptness and the utmost vigour. Hubbard drove the American volunteers and Canadians across the river at the first charge, where they were met by Stickney.

The Rangers alone retired in good order; but Herrick and Nichols having completed their flank movement and driven in all opposing detachments, united at the summit and participated with Stark in storming the breastworks where Baume made a persistent stand and offered real fight. The battle, which began

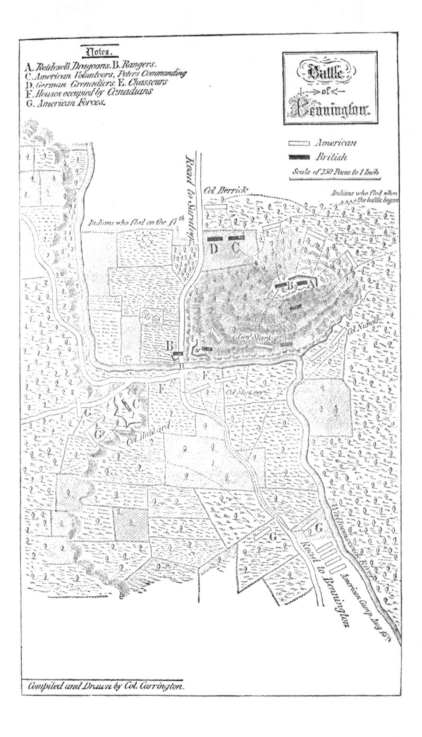

Notes.

A. *Reidesel's Dragoons.* B. *Rangers.*
C. *American Volunteers, Peters Commanding*
D. *German Grenadiers.* E. *Chasseurs*
F. *Houses occupied by Canadians*
G. *American Forces.*

Battle
← of →
Bennington.

American
British
Scale of 250 Paces to 1 Inch.

Road to Sandling.

Col Berrick

Indians who fled when the battle began

Indians who fled on the 14th

D C

D B A

Gen'. Stark.

Col Nichols.

B

F

F *Col Stickney.*

C

G

G *Col Hubbard.*

G G

Walloomsac River.

Road to Bennington.

American Camp Aug 15th.

Compiled and Drawn by Col. Carrington.

about three o clock, was soon over, and many of the militia were engaged in collecting the trophies of the action, when Lieutenant-colonel Breyman's command reached the bridge and attempted to regain the heights. His guns opened fire upon the scattered Americans, and this was the first intimation that they received that the victory was still to be won. The opportune arrival of Colonel Warner s regiment, fresh and in good order, checked the advancing column, and a vigorous action was maintained until the ammunition of the British artillery gave out, and the day closed.

The American trophies included four brass field pieces, twelve brass drums, two hundred and fifty dragoon swords and several hundred stand of arms.

The British casualties are variously stated. Dawson in his *Battles of the United States by Sea and Land*, which is compiled with remark able faithfulness and judgment, adopts Gordon s statement and places the number of killed at two hundred and seven, and the prisoners at seven hundred. Irving states the prisoners at five hundred and fifty-four; Bancroft at six hundred and ninety-two, and Lossing at nine hundred and thirty-four, including the killed and wounded, and one hundred and fifty Tories. This last element must be fully considered, in view of General Burgoyne's official report that "many armed royalists joined the command on the march." It is the only way by which to reconcile the disproportion of casualties to the actual British force which was detailed to Lieutenant-colonel Baume's command.

The Americans lost about forty killed and as many wounded. The killed of the British force must have been mainly from the Canadians and royalists who fled and were shot down by eager pursuers, as nearly four hundred Hessians were among the prisoners captured. Reports of the capture of arms, largely in access of the British force, are predicated upon the idea that these arms were taken with the expedition for distribution to royalists. The *secret* nature of the expedition at the start, and the fact that it was with great difficulty that arms were obtained for six hundred of these recruits, the maximum ever secured by the army, renders such reports untrustworthy.

Thus this battle added its trophies to the gallant fight of Oris-kany and the successful defence of Fort Schuyler. General Stark was promptly promoted by Congress. These events seemed to be the ripe fruit of Washington's prophetic forecast. The militia began at once to hasten to the camp of Schuyler. That officer had been superseded by General Gates, under the direction of the American Congress; but the latter did not arrive to assume command until August nineteenth, just in time to gather laurels already maturing for any discreet commander of the reviving army of the North. General Schuyler received him with cour-tesy, permitted no mortification at this sudden removal from command to chill his enthusiastic support and earnest coopera-tion in securing men and supplies for the prosecution of the campaign; and although not invited by his successor to a council of war which was convened to determine the exact condition of the department, and the necessary measures which its interests demanded, was as loyal to the demands upon his honour and his zeal as if he had been supreme in command, and was about to put on a crown of victory.

LEONAUR

ALSO FROM LEONAUR

AVAILABLE IN SOFTCOVER OR HARDCOVER WITH DUST JACKET

LIFE IN THE ARMY OF NORTHERN VIRGINIA *by Carlton McCarthy*— The Observations of a Confederate Artilleryman of Cutshaw's Battalion During the American Civil War 1861-1865.

HISTORY OF THE CAVALRY OF THE ARMY OF THE POTOMAC *by Charles D. Rhodes*—Including Pope's Army of Virginia and the Cavalry Operations in West Virginia During the American Civil War.

CAMP-FIRE AND COTTON-FIELD *by Thomas W. Knox*—A New York Herald Correspondent's View of the American Civil War.

SERGEANT STILLWELL *by Leander Stillwell* —The Experiences of a Union Army Soldier of the 61st Illinois Infantry During the American Civil War.

STONEWALL'S CANNONEER *by Edward A. Moore*—Experiences with the Rockbridge Artillery, Confederate Army of Northern Virginia, During the American Civil War.

THE SIXTH CORPS *by George Stevens*—The Army of the Potomac, Union Army, During the American Civil War.

THE RAILROAD RAIDERS *by William Pittenger*—An Ohio Volunteers Recollections of the Andrews Raid to Disrupt the Confederate Railroad in Georgia During the American Civil War.

CITIZEN SOLDIER *by John Beatty*—An Account of the American Civil War by a Union Infantry Officer of Ohio Volunteers Who Became a Brigadier General.

COX: PERSONAL RECOLLECTIONS OF THE CIVIL WAR--VOLUME 1 *by Jacob Dolson Cox*—West Virginia, Kanawha Valley, Gauley Bridge, Cotton Mountain, South Mountain, Antietam, the Morgan Raid & the East Tennessee Campaign.

COX: PERSONAL RECOLLECTIONS OF THE CIVIL WAR--VOLUME 2 *by Jacob Dolson Cox*—Siege of Knoxville, East Tennessee, Atlanta Campaign, the Nashville Campaign & the North Carolina Campaign.

KERSHAW'S BRIGADE VOLUME 1 *by D. Augustus Dickert*—Manassas, Seven Pines, Sharpsburg (Antietam), Fredricksburg, Chancellorsville, Gettysburg, Chickamauga, Chattanooga, Fort Sanders & Bean Station.

KERSHAW'S BRIGADE VOLUME 2 *by D. Augustus Dickert*—At the wilderness, Cold Harbour, Petersburg, The Shenandoah Valley and Cedar Creek..

LEONAUR

ALSO FROM LEONAUR

AVAILABLE IN SOFTCOVER OR HARDCOVER WITH DUST JACKET

THE RELUCTANT REBEL *by William G. Stevenson*—A young Kentuckian's experiences in the Confederate Infantry & Cavalry during the American Civil War..

BOOTS AND SADDLES *by Elizabeth B. Custer*—The experiences of General Custer's Wife on the Western Plains.

FANNIE BEERS' CIVIL WAR *by Fannie A. Beers*—A Confederate Lady's Experiences of Nursing During the Campaigns & Battles of the American Civil War.

LADY SALE'S AFGHANISTAN *by Florentia Sale*—An Indomitable Victorian Lady's Account of the Retreat from Kabul During the First Afghan War.

THE TWO WARS OF MRS DUBERLY *by Frances Isabella Duberly*—An Intrepid Victorian Lady's Experience of the Crimea and Indian Mutiny.

THE REBELLIOUS DUCHESS *by Paul F. S. Dermoncourt*—The Adventures of the Duchess of Berri and Her Attempt to Overthrow French Monarchy.

LADIES OF WATERLOO *by Charlotte A. Eaton, Magdalene de Lancey & Juana Smith*—The Experiences of Three Women During the Campaign of 1815: Waterloo Days by Charlotte A. Eaton, A Week at Waterloo by Magdalene de Lancey & Juana's Story by Juana Smith.

TWO YEARS BEFORE THE MAST *by Richard Henry Dana. Jr.*—The account of one young man's experiences serving on board a sailing brig—the Penelope—bound for California, between the years1834-36.

A SAILOR OF KING GEORGE *by Frederick Hoffman*—From Midshipman to Captain—Recollections of War at Sea in the Napoleonic Age 1793-1815.

LORDS OF THE SEA *by A. T. Mahan*—Great Captains of the Royal Navy During the Age of Sail.

COGGESHALL'S VOYAGES: VOLUME 1 *by George Coggeshall*—The Recollections of an American Schooner Captain.

COGGESHALL'S VOYAGES: VOLUME 2 *by George Coggeshall*—The Recollections of an American Schooner Captain.

TWILIGHT OF EMPIRE *by Sir Thomas Ussher & Sir George Cockburn*—Two accounts of Napoleon's Journeys in Exile to Elba and St. Helena: Narrative of Events by Sir Thomas Ussher & Napoleon's Last Voyage: Extract of a diary by Sir George Cockburn.

LEONAUR

ALSO FROM LEONAUR
AVAILABLE IN SOFTCOVER OR HARDCOVER WITH DUST JACKET

IRON TIMES WITH THE GUARDS *by An O. E. (G. P. A. Fildes)*—The Experiences of an Officer of the Coldstream Guards on the Western Front During the First World War.

THE GREAT WAR IN THE MIDDLE EAST: 1 *by W. T. Massey*—The Desert Campaigns & How Jerusalem Was Won---two classic accounts in one volume.

THE GREAT WAR IN THE MIDDLE EAST: 2 *by W. T. Massey*—Allenby's Final Triumph.

SMITH-DORRIEN *by Horace Smith-Dorrien*—Isandlwhana to the Great War.

1914 *by Sir John French*—The Early Campaigns of the Great War by the British Commander.

GRENADIER *by E. R. M. Fryer*—The Recollections of an Officer of the Grenadier Guards throughout the Great War on the Western Front.

BATTLE, CAPTURE & ESCAPE *by George Pearson*—The Experiences of a Canadian Light Infantryman During the Great War.

DIGGERS AT WAR *by R. Hugh Knyvett & G. P. Cuttriss*—"Over There" With the Australians by R. Hugh Knyvett and Over the Top With the Third Australian Division by G. P. Cuttriss. Accounts of Australians During the Great War in the Middle East, at Gallipoli and on the Western Front.

HEAVY FIGHTING BEFORE US *by George Brenton Laurie*—The Letters of an Officer of the Royal Irish Rifles on the Western Front During the Great War.

THE CAMELIERS *by Oliver Hogue*—A Classic Account of the Australians of the Imperial Camel Corps During the First World War in the Middle East.

RED DUST *by Donald Black*—A Classic Account of Australian Light Horsemen in Palestine During the First World War.

THE LEAN, BROWN MEN *by Angus Buchanan*—Experiences in East Africa During the Great War with the 25th Royal Fusiliers—the Legion of Frontiersmen.

THE NIGERIAN REGIMENT IN EAST AFRICA *by W. D. Downes*—On Campaign During the Great War 1916-1918.

THE 'DIE-HARDS' IN SIBERIA *by John Ward*—With the Middlesex Regiment Against the Bolsheviks 1918-19.

LEONAUR

ALSO FROM LEONAUR

AVAILABLE IN SOFTCOVER OR HARDCOVER WITH DUST JACKET

THE 9TH—THE KING'S (LIVERPOOL REGIMENT) IN THE GREAT WAR 1914 - 1918 *by Enos H. G. Roberts*—Mersey to mud—war and Liverpool men.

THE GAMBARDIER *by Mark Severn*—The experiences of a battery of Heavy artillery on the Western Front during the First World War.

FROM MESSINES TO THIRD YPRES *by Thomas Floyd*—A personal account of the First World War on the Western front by a 2/5th Lancashire Fusilier.

THE IRISH GUARDS IN THE GREAT WAR - VOLUME 1 *by Rudyard Kipling*—Edited and Compiled from Their Diaries and Papers—The First Battalion.

THE IRISH GUARDS IN THE GREAT WAR - VOLUME 1 *by Rudyard Kipling*—Edited and Compiled from Their Diaries and Papers—The Second Battalion.

ARMOURED CARS IN EDEN *by K. Roosevelt*—An American President's son serving in Rolls Royce armoured cars with the British in Mesopatamia & with the American Artillery in France during the First World War.

CHASSEUR OF 1914 *by Marcel Dupont*—Experiences of the twilight of the French Light Cavalry by a young officer during the early battles of the great war in Europe.

TROOP HORSE & TRENCH *by R.A. Lloyd*—The experiences of a British Lifeguardsman of the household cavalry fighting on the western front during the First World War 1914-18.

THE EAST AFRICAN MOUNTED RIFLES *by C.J. Wilson*—Experiences of the campaign in the East African bush during the First World War.

THE LONG PATROL *by George Berrie*—A Novel of Light Horsemen from Gallipoli to the Palestine campaign of the First World War.

THE FIGHTING CAMELIERS *by Frank Reid*—The exploits of the Imperial Camel Corps in the desert and Palestine campaigns of the First World War.

STEEL CHARIOTS IN THE DESERT *by S. C. Rolls*—The first world war experiences of a Rolls Royce armoured car driver with the Duke of Westminster in Libya and in Arabia with T.E. Lawrence.

WITH THE IMPERIAL CAMEL CORPS IN THE GREAT WAR *by Geoffrey Inchbald*—The story of a serving officer with the British 2nd battalion against the Senussi and during the Palestine campaign.

AVAILABLE ONLINE AT **www.leonaur.com**
AND FROM ALL GOOD BOOK STORES
07/09

9 780857 064745